To Jill and Robin —
        Such dear friends
Such great educators!

        With all love,

                Kate

SHAKESPEARE'S EDUCATION

How Shakespeare Learned to Write

Kate Pogue

Kate Emery Pogue

America Star Books

First printing

America Star Books has allowed this work to remain exactly as the author intended, verbatim, without editorial input.

Hardcover 9781632499356
Softcover 9781462678709
PUBLISHED BY AMERICA STAR BOOKS, LLLP
www.americastarbooks.com

Printed in the United States of America

TO JOAN

IN GRATITUDE FOR HER ALWAYS
GENEROUS AND ENTHUSIASTIC SUPPORT

ACKNOWLEDGMENTS

I am indebted to many friends and colleagues for their help in the creation of this book. Ann Christensen, Jean DeWitt, Peter Greenfield, Jane Cowling, and Emma Taylor read all or parts of the book and gave invaluable suggestions. Ed Cueva translated Latin that would otherwise have remained obscure for me and for my readers. Robert Simpson and Bruce Power of Christ Church Cathedral, Houston, were of help in exploring musical education in Tudor times.

Librarians Laura Stalker and Stephen Tabor helped maximize my time at the Huntington Library, while Kathleen Lynch and Carol Brobeck at the Folger Library encouraged me with their enthusiasm for this project. At the Dykes Library at University of Houston Downtown the librarians, especially Lore Guilmartin, were exceptionally helpful.

I am grateful for the support of colleagues in Stratford-Upon-Avon. Robert Bearman's critique of the text saved me from important technical errors, and his recommendation of Norma Hampson at the Shakespeare Birthplace Trust (SBT) enabled me to access materials there, even from Houston, Texas. Thank you to Bob, Norma, and the always-helpful SBT. John Taplin shared generously his expertise on Shakespeare's family life and took time to give critiques of this manuscript, while Richard Pearson and David Biddle helped me feel in touch with the long history of the King Edward VI School of which they are so important a part.

Paul Dupree, David Peterson, Jerilyn Watson, Pat Laing, David Yarham, Jill and Robin Lunn, and my brother and sister-in-law, Robert and Ann Emery, welcomed me into their homes when I travelled to do research. They made me feel working on this book was indistinguishable from vacation and pure pleasure. Other friends whose support I treasure include Niki Flacks, Scott Williams, Jim Glenn, Charles and Chesley Krohn, and Liz and Howard Ayers. Kathleen Vander Meer caringly reviewed the text, and her editorial notes always began with a reminder to keep my reader in mind.

I want to thank my family for their patience and encouragement, especially Joan, to whom this book is dedicated, and my niece, Daisy Hagey, who was kind enough to proofread the manuscript.

And most of all, I am grateful to Mike McClory. The book would not be as it is without his profound understanding of the tangled history of the English language and his insightful, painstaking editing.

CONTENTS

SHAKESPEARE'S EDUCATION

How Shakespeare Learned to Write

Kate Emery Pogue

FOREWORD

Imagine an hourglass. Every grain of sand in the upper globe is a bit of information about schools in 16th century England; every grain in the lower globe is a word, a phrase, or a line in a Shakespearean play or poem referring to his education and upbringing. Each of these passed through the neck of the hourglass: the King Edward VI School in Stratford. What young William Shakespeare learned at that school, and how he learned it, is the subject of this book.

The thousands of grains of sand in the upper globe reflect the sources of information that exist concerning education in Tudor and Jacobean England. It is challenging, even daunting, to try to read comprehensively in this field. Educational theory was written about in depth and detail from the Middle Ages through the reforms instituted under Henry VIII, Edward VI, and Elizabeth I. During this tumultuous era, England witnessed the founding of hundreds of schools with prescribed statutes and curricula, and dozens of teachers recorded their experiences.

Almost all biographies of Shakespeare give a page or two—or at times a chapter—to his schooldays, the outlines of which are sketchy but well known. All of them quote lines from his plays and trace their origins, where relevant, to Shakespeare's education. But my interest is different. I have been eager to discover the daily routines of Shakespeare the schoolboy in order to make his academic experiences come to life. I am interested in both the content of his education and the way it was transmitted—

in how he learned as well as what he learned—because I am convinced that both were essential to his later work as a poet and playwright.

From the mid-20th century on, one could not dream of discussing Shakespeare's education without reference to the massive work of T. W. Baldwin. First, in *Shakspere's Petty School* (1943), Baldwin goes into detail concerning the pre-school system in Tudor England. In *Shakspere's Small Latine and Lesse Greeke* (1944) and *Shakspere's Five-Act Structure (1947),* he describes the founding of the English grammar school system, its curricula, the great teachers who created it and the books they taught. The amount of detail in Baldwin is so crushing, however, that even the most sophisticated scholar can get lost. Easier to absorb are A. Monroe Stowe's *English Grammar Schools in the Reign of Queen Elizabeth* (1908); Foster Watson's *The Curriculum and Text-books of English Schools in the First Half of the Seventeenth Century* (1903), *The English Grammar Schools to 1660* (1908), *Tudor School Boy Life* (1908), and *Vives on Education* (1913); as well as John Brown's *Elizabethan Schooldays* and George A. Plimpton's *The Education of Shakespeare,* both published in 1933.

The dates of these books, and the recent cascade of conspiracy theories claiming that Shakespeare did not have enough education to write his plays, impel us to take a fresh look at Shakespeare's schooling.

This book invites all those fascinated with Shakespeare to travel in imagination back to late sixteenth-century England, to compare their own schooldays with the experiences of Tudor schoolboys, and to observe the impact of Shakespeare's education on his dramatic and poetic work.

INTRODUCTION

When Henry VIII focused his powerful intelligence on changing the course of the English educational system, he surely did not intend it to be a training ground for playwrights—but it was.

His primary goals were to unify religious belief in his country, to change the language of the church from Latin to English (while retaining Latin as the official language of the schools) and to develop an educated society trained to embrace the new humanist ways of thinking. Henry turned for help to the great educational philosophers of the age, among them the Dutch scholar Desiderius Erasmus and the English bishop, John Colet, Dean of St. Paul's Cathedral and founder of St. Paul's School. The records left by these men—the king, the scholar, and the cleric—show how they intended to move England's Cathedral-based English system of education away from the scholasticism of the Middle Ages and into the new classicism of the Renaissance.

Henry and his cohorts envisioned a system that was to be uniform. It would apply to the entire spectrum of English schools: to very ancient schools claiming dates of establishment as far back as the Norman conquest and beyond—St. Peter's York (627), Warwick (914), St. Albans (948), and Bedford (a relative newcomer in 1085); as well as to the great cathedral schools—schools whose names ring out like the great bells in their church towers: Chester, Ely, Gloucester, Peterborough, Rochester, Worcester, Bristol, Wells, Hereford, Salisbury. It would shape the public schools, founded to widen access to education beyond the country's elite (who could afford private tutors): schools such as Eton, Winchester College, Ipswich, Charterhouse, Sherborne, Merchant Taylors', Harrow, Rugby, Shrewsbury and Christ College, Brecon; and determine the curriculum of the town grammar schools as well.

The push went beyond Henry's reign. Over a hundred new and compliant town schools were added or renamed in the time of Henry's son Edward VI, including Shakespeare's school, the King Edward VI School (called the Kynges Newe Schole in the town's charter of 1553), and more schools were established in the age of Elizabeth. But it was Henry's determination to remodel the system that provided the impetus for uniformity—of standards, curriculum, textbooks, even schedules—in schools throughout the country.[1]

Here's how the system worked. At age four or five, children of both sexes were to go to petty school to learn their letters and to learn how to read religious works, such as the Lord's Prayer and the Catechism, in English. The ability to read the *Bible* and prayer books in the vernacular gave citizens direct access to religious texts. This aided Henry in his desire to lessen the control the Catholic Church held over the minds of the people. No longer would Latin-speaking priests alone wield the power to interpret sacred texts—to tell people what the words meant and what they were to believe.

---

1   Though uniformity was the goal, it was not easily achieved. Richard Mulcaster, a visionary educator of the time, pleaded for greater uniformity in the training of teachers, so that good methods would prevail, and more uniformity in the choice of texts, which left much decision-making to the individual instructor. He comments on how a lack of uniformity in texts worked a hardship on students and parents: "the parentes purses are pretily pulled, and the poor men very sore pinched both with change of books, the master oft repealing his former choice..."

But as students went from petty school to grammar school (boys only from this point on), their English studies ceased. Now they had to learn to read, write, and speak in Latin, for Latin was the language of civilized people throughout Europe, and fluency in Latin was a prerequisite for young men hoping to rise in Tudor England's upwardly mobile society. So the boys in school had to learn how to analyze and construct sentences using more than 150 Latinate figures of speech. They memorized these figures, then went on to learn aphorisms and to write themes based on them. They studied the works of the great classical writers, Cicero and Ovid among them, and constructed orations, speaking first in one person's voice, then in another's. They mastered Latin grammar (as well as a little Greek), logic, rhetoric, and they practiced music and penmanship. What's more, as a critical part of their learning, they memorized roles and performed in plays, where they were enjoined to stand up straight, gesture appropriately, and speak forcefully. They attended school six days a week (seven at some of the residence schools) from dawn to dusk. Out of this rigorous system, out of thousands of highly literate graduates, came some three-dozen men who, in the late 1500s and early 1600s, applied their education to the writing of plays, and who created one of the world's great theatrical eras.

Shakespeare was one of these writers. Although we have no records from the King Edward VI School, we know a great deal about other schools in England's emerging system of uniform education. And what we know shows that the curriculum, the schedule, and the requirements for teaching in the grammar schools -- following the royal mandates of Henry, Edward, and Elizabeth, along with the early influence of Erasmus, Colet, and their colleague

William Lily—were standardized. To learn about William Shakespeare's education, we need to look closely at examples provided by other schools of the time, among them the schools attended by his great contemporaries Thomas Kyd, Christopher Marlowe, and Ben Jonson. These three young men and William Shakespeare may have grown up in different parts of the country, but when writing their plays in London, they drew upon a common educational experience. All of them received instruction from well-educated and thoughtful teachers; put in long, demanding hours of study based on Latin classics and the Bible; and benefitted from a curriculum that encouraged frequent recitation and the performance of plays by students.

To understand Shakespeare's education, we need to look at how the school days were organized, what subjects the students encountered at each level (forms), and how Shakespeare learned at an early age the skills he applied in composing the great works of his maturity.

CHAPTER 1

PETTY SCHOOL AND SCHOOLMASTERS

> "Let the school be made unto them a place of play:
> and the children drawn on by that pleasant delight
> which ought to be, it can then no more hinder their
> growth than their play doth, but rather further it,
> when they sit at their ease..."[2]

At age four or five, young William Shakespeare—as the son of a prosperous, though undereducated, businessman—would have begun his studies at a local petty school (literally, "little" school), essentially a combination of what we would call pre-school and kindergarten. The "petties" were not formal schools in the sense that we use the term today. They were operated more or less as sidelines by reasonably literate people engaged in a variety of occupations—a parish clerk, or a tailor, a weaver, a seamstress.[3] Virtually anyone who could read and write,

---

2.   Brinsley, *Ludus Literarius: or, The Grammar Schoole*, 10. Note: Throughout this book, I have chosen to modernize spelling when a quote is lengthy and/or when the original spelling makes a quotation difficult to read. I have kept the antique spelling when it causes no difficulty in reading and when it adds to the flavor or authenticity of the citation. Spelling had not become standardized in the Tudor age. There is wide variation in the spelling of many names (Shakespeare's included) and other familiar words.

3.   See Francis Clement, *The Petie Schole* (1587):
To the Little Children
Come, little child, let toys alone
And trifles in the street:
Come, get thee to the parish clark
It is made a Teacher meet.
Frequent ye now the Taylor's shop
And eeke the Weavers lamb:
There's neither these, but can with skill
Them teach that thither come,
The semistresse she (a Mistress now)
Hath lore as much to read
As erst she had in many years

it would seem, could open a petty school. In Stratford we know by name a man "who taught the children reading and writing while his wife taught needlework."[4] They, and many others in towns across the country, taught the ABCs, the forming of letters into words and words into sentences, the reading of familiar stories and required religious texts, the "casting of accounts" (an approach to basic arithmetic), and sometimes the rudiments of Latin.

Shakespeare in Stratford, his contemporaries Christopher Marlowe in Canterbury, Ben Jonson in Westminster, Thomas Kyd in London, all faced the same requirements for boys wanting to enter grammar school: "None shall be admitted a scholar before he is seven years old...such only are to be received into our school who have thoroughly learnt by heart at least the eight [Latin] parts of speech and know how to write at least moderately well."[5] The system was set up to ensure that the students would be ready to progress through seven challenging years in grammar school before graduation at 14 or 15.

So, at age seven, armed with the Latin parts of speech and able to read and write in English, Shakespeare—like Marlowe, Jonson, and Kyd—started grammar school, setting out at dawn from the family's house on Henley Street. Imagine him as a little boy, satchel in hand, off to

---

Compast by silk and thread.
I cannot all by name rehearse
For many more you see
Come, make your choice, let toys alone
And trifles: Learn A, B.

4.   Chute, *Shakespeare of London*, 13. Robert Bearman notes that this teacher, Thomas Parker, had been around Stratford from at least 1592 according to the *Minutes and Accounts of the Stratford Corporation* 6 306-7.

5.   Baldwin, *William Shakspere's Small Latine and Lesse Greek*, 1:381, quoting A. F. Leach's *Educational Charters and Documents*.

school like his life-long friends Richard Quiney, Richard Field, Richard Tyler, and Hamnet Sadler, making his way across town to Stratford's Guild Hall. By six o'clock an assistant schoolmaster (called the usher)[6] had arrived, and the long day began. At seven, the Schoolmaster, or pedagogue, in his scholar's hat, black gown flapping, came in to take the upper forms to the front of the classroom, while the lower forms studied in the back with the usher.

The forty or so boys attending Stratford's King Edward VI School[7] were divided into forms based on age and mastery of the subject matter. Hour by hour and term by term, the boys worked their way through a sequence of lessons focused on mastering Latin and working with the classical literature written in that ancient language. By the Third Form (about half way through their schooling, when the boys were 10 or 11) they were required to speak Latin everywhere, not just in the classroom.

Richard Mulcaster, first headmaster of the Merchant Taylors' School in London, and playwright Thomas Kyd's teacher, argued for English instruction in schools. But despite his impassioned pleas for the vernacular, most schools taught English very little—the primary objective of the uniform curriculum that Shakespeare grew up with was the mastery of Latin.

---

6.   Though often the ushers were unknown, according to Eccles, 52, the assistant teacher from time to time (including the 1560s and '70s) seems to have been the curate, William Gilbert, alias Higgs.

7.   The exact number of students in any given year cannot be determined, only approximated, given the population of the town and the size of the school room. Though the number of students would vary from year to year, it was not a large school at this time.

In grammar school, the gentle, cheerful petty school experience gave way to a harsher reality. Young Romeo may have been expressing Shakespeare's own feelings when he observed "Love goes toward love like schoolboys from their books/ But love from love toward school with heavy looks." In his early *Two Gentlemen of Verona*, Shakespeare recalled what it's like "To sigh, like a schoolboy that had lost his ABC." Later, in As You Like It, he had Jaques describe "...the whining schoolboy, with his satchel/ And shining morning face creeping like snail/ Unwillingly to school..."[8] And the schoolmaster, in *Love's Labour's Lost*, was presented as "A domineering pedant o'er the boy, / Than whom no mortal so magnificent."

The schoolmaster, then, was a figure to be feared as well as respected. Some clues as to why can be seen in woodcuts of the time: a famous one shows the schoolmaster wielding a birch, his switch made of a branch with a broom-like profusion of smaller branches and twigs, whipping the bared backside of a failing student.[9]

Though flogging boys was the norm, and was often vicious, not all schoolmasters were rough. Not Mulcaster, and certainly not Roger Ascham, the tutor to Elizabeth I. Ascham said in *The Scholemaster,* "I assure you, there is no such whetstone to sharpen a good wit and encourage a

---

8.   In the satchel carried by *As You Like It's* whining boy were often bread and butter and fruit for breakfast (the boys arrived too early to have eaten); quills and a penknife; an inkhorn or inkwell; books; paper, a ruler and blotting paper or sand canisters; tables (what we might call a tablet); pencils or a silverpoint stylus and books as needed—equipment for hard mental work. In addition the boys often brought a candle for the dark early morning hours and a contribution to the fuel for the brazier in the winter.

9.   Riggs, 47; Wood, 51. In *Shakespeare's Schoolroom,* Lynn Enterline makes a powerful argument for the underlying erotic dimension of the ubiquitous flogging and how this was expressed in the literature of the time.

will to learning, as is praise."[10] And Mulcaster thoughtfully weighted the values of praise and punishment; "For Gentleness and courtesy toward children, I do think it more needful than beating, and ever to be wished, because it implies a good nature in the child, which is any parent's comfort, any master's delight."[11]

This was not just sentimental theory, for Mulcaster claimed: "Myself have had thousands under my hand, whom I never beat, neither they ever much needed. But," he continued, "if the rod had not been in sight, and assured them of punishment if they had swerved too much, they would have deserved [beating]."[12]

There is no record of undue cruelty in the schoolmasters who taught Shakespeare; they were educators first, perhaps, and disciplinarians second. We have the names of all of them, beginning with the town charter in 1553—and while the first had the propitious name of William Smart, the most important teachers during Shakespeare's years at school were Simon Hunt and Thomas Jenkins.

Offering quite decent pay (20 pounds per annum), Stratford attracted good teachers—though often did not keep them long.[13] Walter Roche became master of the grammar school in Stratford a few years before Shakespeare was admitted. Roche had a BA from Oxford and Queen Elizabeth had

10.   Baldwin, *Shakspere's Small Latine* 1: 265.
11.   Mulcaster, *Positions,* 278-80.
12.   Ibid.
13.   During Shakespeare's time at school the schoolmasters remained only three or four years before going on to other work. Shortly after Shakespeare left school, however, the job of schoolmaster was given to Alexander Aspinall who remained at the post for forty-two years. Aspinall married a wealthy widow, became a businessman as well as teacher, and was the only friend of Shakespeare's who was also an academic. See Pogue, *Shakespeare's Friends.*

made him rector of Droitwich,[14] a town near Stratford. Hunt replaced Roche in 1671, and by the time Shakespeare moved on to the upper school there was yet another new master: Thomas Jenkins.

Jenkins was born about 1548 into a poor family in London. However his father was a servant of Sir Thomas White who founded St. John's College, Oxford. Thomas was a gifted scholar. He graduated from St. John's, Oxford, took a master's degree, and was a fellow there from 1566-1572, shortly before coming to Stratford (1575-1579). These were Shakespeare's last four years at school, and Jenkins necessarily played a major role in the most sophisticated part of his education. As St. John's College emphasized Greek in its curriculum, Jenkins would have likely included Greek studies for his advanced students in Stratford—from him, Shakespeare would have learned the "lesse Greeke" Ben Jonson cited so scornfully.

---

14.   Wellstood, ed. *3*:23, 1921. Roche was presented with the living at Droitwich on 29 November 1569, thus he held the rectorship of Droitwich and the mastership of Stratford grammar school simultaneously. Droitwich is said to be the home of John Hemming's father, leading to the thought that Shakespeare might have been acquainted with this gifted actor and theatre manager (and later good friend) before going to London.

CHAPTER 2

THE SCHOOL DAY

As has been true since formal education began, the teaching experience and the temperament of each Tudor schoolmaster determined how he would present the materials of a fixed curriculum to his students.

But however different the personality of the masters might have been, and however much their choice of books, say, might have varied, the structure set forth by Henry, Edward and Elizabeth mandated many universal routines. The Canterbury records tell us at what hour the usher and schoolmaster began work at Christopher Marlowe's school; many other school records indicate the same hours for their teachers.

> "Item: that usher shall every day enter the school by six of the clock and the schoolmaster by seven, there to continue until eight of the clock be stricken, and then to go at their liberty until nine of the clock, and then to return and so continue till eleven of the clock; and at one of the clock they shall return again to the school and there continue till three, and then to go at their liberty till four of the clock, and then to return and there continue till five...".[15]

The records of the public school Eton and the town school at Hawkeshead provide more details.[16] At Eton in 1560, for instance, the days Monday through Thursday kept to an identical schedule. Work began at six a.m. with the usher commanding the boys to kneel. Young scholars across the

---

15.   Baldwin, *Shakespere's Small Latine*, 1: 168, *Visitation Articles and Injunctions of the Period of the Reformation.*
16.   Ibid., Chapter 15, 353-79.

country were obligated to begin their day with prayers, prayers that exerted an important influence on the writing style of the time. They were made up of long sentences that built complex syntax and rhythmic components into young minds; and they were repeated more than a thousand times over the course of seven years. Imagine each and every morning a schoolroom of boys reciting:

> "Most mighty God, and merciful father, we sinners by nature, yet thy Children by grace, here prostrate before thy divine Majesty, do acknowledge our Corruption in nature, by reason of our sin to be such, that we are not able as of ourselves to think one good thought much less able to profit in good learning and literature, and to come to the knowledge of thy son Christ our savior, except it shall please thee of thy great grace and goodness to illuminate our understanding, to strengthen our feeble memories, to instruct us by thy holy spirit, and so pour upon us thy good gifts of grace, that we may learn to know to practice those things in these our studies, as may most tend to the glory of thy name, to the profit of thy Church, and to the performance of our Christian duty, Hear us O God, grant this our Petition, and bless our studies O heavenly father, for thy son Jesus Christ's sake, in whose name we call upon thee, and say Our father... "[17]

The students would then continue with the Lord's Prayer.[18]

---

17. Stowe, 154. This was the prayer required by Statute for the boys in school at Hawkeshead. It was approved by Bishop Sands, the Archbishop of York. The prayers at Stratford, if not identical, would have been similar.

18. The text of the Lord's Prayer in the *Book of Common Prayer* 1559 (the Elizabethan prayer book) reads:
    "Our Father, which art in heaven, hallowed by thy name. Thy kingdom come. Thy will be done in earth as it is in heaven. Give us this day our daily bread. And forgive us our trespasses, as we forgive those who trespass against us. And lead us not into temptation. But deliver us from evil. Amen."
    The familiar ending "For thine is the kingdom and the power and the glory for ever and ever. Amen" appears in the *English Book of Common Prayer* beginning with the revision of 1662.

When Shakespeare used intricate sentence structures in his plays, his actors were accustomed to phrasing them and his audiences were used to following their tortuous but familiar patterns. All ears would be searching for the meaning and the pleasure found in rhythmic repetition.

The dramatic rhythms of four: "*to illuminate* our understanding, *to strengthen* our feeble memories, *to instruct* us by thy holy spirit, *and so pour upon us* thy good gifts of grace…" and three: "as may most tend *to the glory* of thy name, *to the profit* of thy Church, and *to the performance* of our Christian duty," were taught as linguistic tropes, reinforced in the rhetoric of the time, and are clearly echoed in Shakespeare's work, as in his construction of Brutus's oration following the assassination of Julius Caesar.

BRUTUS:

Romans, countrymen, and lovers! *hear me* for my cause, and be silent, that you may hear: *believe me* for mine honour, and have respect to mine honour, that you may believe: *censure me* in your wisdom, and awake your senses, that you may the better judge. *(Rhythm of three: tricolon)*…

As Caesar loved me, I weep for him; *as he was fortunate*, I rejoice at it; *as he was valiant*, I honour him: but, *as he was ambitious*, I slew him. *(Rhythm of four)*

There is tears for his love; joy for his fortune; honour for his valour; and death for his ambition. *(Rhythm of four)*

Who is here so base that would be a bondman? *If any, speak; for him have I offended.* Who is here so rude that would not be a Roman? *If any, speak; for him have I offended.* Who is here so vile that will not love his country? *If any, speak; for him have I offended. (Rhythm of three: tricolon)*

Julius Caesar, Act III Scene 2[19]

The statutes of many schools of the time stipulated that boys attend school regularly, be on time, and be apt scholars or they risked dismissal. At St. Alban's, the rules said: "Ye shall see diligently from time to time, that your child keep duely the ordinary hours and times in coming to school. If your child be absent above three days in a Quarter (except he be sick) then he shall be banished the school. If your child shall prove unapt for learning, then upon warning thereof given, ye shall take him away."[20]

So, after morning prayers, the usher took the roll. When the usher called a boy's name, the student answered "*adsum*,"[21] "I am present." Thus his long day of Latin began.

After roll, according to the Eton calendar, the usher examined the boys' faces and hands for cleanliness; later, the students would have to show them again to the schoolmaster. (Shakespeare described the schoolboy with "his shining morning face,"[22] scrubbed by his mother so he could pass this daily examination.)

Next, it was on to Lily's *Latin Grammar* and hard study began; endless verbs were waiting to be conjugated and nouns to be declined.

At seven a.m. the students had a short break for breakfast or a snack, brought from home in the students' satchels.

---

19.   Abraham Lincoln would echo these rhythms in the Gettysburg Address, referencing both Shakespeare and his classical sources. These oratorical devices continued to pattern English until the twentieth century.
20.   Stowe, 132.
21.   *King Edward VI School*, 13.
22.   *As You Like It*, Act II Scene 7.

Then the upper forms were taken by the schoolmaster, who once again made certain all students were present. At this time, the students recited by memory exercises they had been given the day before.

At eight a.m. came the *sententiae.*

Leonard Culman's *Sententiae Pueriles* was the first book other than Lily from which children learned their Latin. It listed as *sententiae* such simple phrases in Latin as: "Help thy friends." "Abstain from other folks' things." "Conceal a secret thing." "Be thou affable in speech." "Prove thy friends." Gradually, as the boys progressed, the phrases lengthened from two Latin words to three, four and longer.

The usher introduced students to these pithy moral sayings first in order simply to translate them (in the First through Fourth Forms). But the master used them in different ways for each subsequent form: in the Fifth Form *sententiae* were to be varied, in the Sixth they were to be used as subjects for themes and then for early efforts at versifying. If there were a Seventh and Eighth Form (as in large schools, or schools which had especially able boys) they were the subjects of the boys' efforts at debate and rhetoric.

Sententiae were employed so intensively that they necessarily had an effect on the writing style of the time. The most famous echo in Shakespeare's work is found in the advice Polonius gave Laertes in *Hamlet,* as the young man set off for Paris. Shakespeare showed Polonius unable to express himself except through the memorized aphorisms from his long-past schooldays. The relentless sequence of them showed Shakespeare was ever ready to mock linguistic conventions as he recalled his education. The phrases I've italicized mirror the *sententiae*.

POLONIUS:

> Give every man thy ear, but few thy voice;
> Take each man's censure, but reserve thy judgment.
> Costly thy habit as thy purse can buy,
> But not express'd in fancy; rich, not gaudy;
> For the apparel oft proclaims the man...
> Neither a borrower nor a lender be;
> For loan oft loses both itself and friend,
> And borrowing dulls the edge of husbandry.
> This above all: to thine own self be true,
> And it must follow, as the night the day,
> Thou canst not then be false to any man.
> (*Hamlet*, Act I Scene 3)

In *Twelfth Night,* Sir Toby Belch recalled a *sententia* from his youth when, toward the end of a debauched evening, he reminded Sir Andrew Aguecheek: "*Diluculo sugere...*" part of a Latin aphorism meaning "it is most healthy to rise early": *Diluculo surgere, saluberrimum est,* found on page 20 of Lily's *Latin Grammar.* Another, in Act IV of *Love's Labour's Lost: Vir sapit, qui pauca loquetur* ("It is a wise man who speaks little"), came from the same source.

Following work on the *sententiae*, the day continued as follows:

9 a.m.   Figures of Speech: Latin figures to be recognized, practiced (Lower School)

Memory work: declensions, conjugations, vocabulary, dialogues (all forms)

Themes: the writing of essays based on a moral idea (Upper School)

Versification: turning prose passages into verse, and the opposite (Upper School)

10 a.m.   Rise for prayers

11 a.m.   Process to hall for dinner (students at Stratford would go home for dinner)

Noon   Parts of speech from *Lily's Latin Grammar*

1 p.m.   Examination by the Master of Upper Forms on Latin speaking

Themes written for teacher critiques

3 p.m.   Break for exercise[23]

4 p.m.   Fourth Form: figures of Grammar

Fifth Form: the writing of epistles based on Cicero (also called Tully from his middle name) using the figures and tropes from Susenbrotus.

Sixth and Seventh Forms: Greek Grammar

---

23.   Richard Mulcaster, in *Positions Concerning the Bringing Up of Children* (1581), recommended exercises intended to keep children fit and healthy. His exercises included wrestling, fencing, swimming, riding, hunting, shooting, and (perhaps surprisingly) singing, dancing, laughing, weeping and holding one's breath. Reading and loud speaking were included, an example of how the children were being trained for effective public performance.

On Fridays the schedule changed. This was the day for discipline, corrections and punishments. After these were meted out, the Saturday assignments were made.

On Saturdays at 7 a.m., Friday's homework recitations were heard; at 9 a.m. came a welcome break. Returning at 1 pm, the boys reviewed the week's work and then took part in debates.

After 3 p.m. on Saturdays, boys in the town grammar schools would be free at last to play or to go home.

CHAPTER 3

THE LOWER SCHOOL CURRICULUM

As Shakespeare moved through the lower forms of King Edward VI School, both what he learned and how he learned it had a discernable influence on the content and form of his plays. Latin in general, and Lily's *Grammar* in particular, lay at the heart of the Tudor educational system, but the boys' physical appearance and manners also received close attention. Upon entering the Lower School, the boys were taught to be circumspect in their manner and in the condition of their attire. Edward Coote made this concern the theme of a well-known verse of the time:

The Schoolmaster to his Scholars

My child and scholar, take good heed,
Unto the words which here are set:
And see you do accordingly,
Or else be sure you shall be beat.

First, I command thee God to serve
Then to thy parents duty yield.
Unto all men be duteous,
And mannerly in town and field.

Your clothes unbuttoned do not use,
Let not your hose ungartered be:
Have handkerchief in readiness,
Wash hands and face, or see not me.

Lose not your books, ink horn nor pen,
Nor girdle, garters, hat nor band:

Let shoes be tied, pin shirt band close,
Keep well your points at any hand.[24]

What constituted appropriate attire was clearly understood by Shakespeare's audiences who heard Ophelia's description of the maddened Hamlet and shared her stunned reaction:

My lord, as I was sewing in my closet,
Lord Hamlet with his doublet all unbraced,
No hat upon his head, his stockings fouled,
Ungart'red, and down-gyved to his ankle,
Pale as his shirt, his knees knocking each other,
And with a look so piteous in purport
As if he had been loosed out of hell,
To speak of horrors – he comes before me.

Hamlet Act II Scene 1

The boys in the lower school were taught at an early age that to be careless in dress was a vice. What's more, cleanliness, and formal dress and manners were a signal to the boys to be prepared for disciplined study. Young as they were, they would now have to concentrate on the demanding techniques fundamental to the Tudor system.

In Tudor times, the school curriculum revolved around calling on each boy to prove orally his gradual mastery of Latin. The exercises in the first three forms involved analyzing the language (by construing and parsing); imitating, memorizing, and then reciting; and turning.

---

24   Coote, 63. "Points" refers to the laces that tied a boy's hose or pants to his doublet.
The poem finishes:
If broken hosed or shooed you go,
Or slovenly in your array:
Without a girdle, or untrust,
Then you and I must make a fray.

ANALYZING, IMITATING, MEMORIZING, AND RECITING

The initial questioning of the boys was based on the analytical techniques of construing and parsing—that is, asking them to take apart and analyze a Latin sentence (construing) and to describe the form, part of speech, and function of each word (parsing). These techniques were based on the theory that all education should start with analysis and imitation, for it was by analyzing and imitating the best writers that the boys would master the moral subjects they studied and the Latin language in which the great classical ideas were expressed.

First Form (ages 7-8):

Students were to study the *Accidence* (the first part of Lily's *Latin Grammar*) as far as the rules of construction; before they could construct sentences, they had to learn to analyze them via the parts of speech. Having identified nouns and verbs, they were to do exercises in declining and conjugating them.

Second Form (ages 8-9):

Students were set to work on the rules of sentence construction. For example, they would read from Cato's *Maxims* in order to observe a well-constructed sentence; then they were to create one in imitation. These exercises were called "making Latins," which simply meant translating phrases and sentences from English into Latin. The boys also started their work on the *Sententiae Pueriles,* which "they repeated by heart, and construed, and parsed."[25]

CATECHIZING

Third Form (ages 9-10):

From the earliest forms the students were catechized: they were given a rule of grammar—a verb to conjugate, a noun to decline, a principle to memorize—and were called upon by the usher, one by one, to recite what they had learned. Shakespeare gave us an example in the scene between schoolmaster Hugh Evans and young William Page in *The Merry Wives of Windsor.*

SIR HUGH EVANS

What is 'fair,' William? (asking for the Latin translation)

WILLIAM PAGE

Pulcher...

SIR HUGH EVANS

What is 'lapis,' William?

WILLIAM PAGE

A stone.

SIR HUGH EVANS

And what is 'a stone,' William?

WILLIAM PAGE

---

25.   Adams, 58, quoting Hoole.

A pebble.(William mistakenly gives a synonym when a "turn" back to Latin is required.)

SIR HUGH EVANS

No, it is 'lapis:' I pray you, remember in your brain.

WILLIAM PAGE

Lapis.[26]

In *Henry IV Part 1,* Shakespeare had Falstaff catechize himself in his famous speech on "honour." Referring to the death (debt) he owed God, he says:

FALSTAFF:

'Tis not due yet; I would be loath to pay him before

his day. What need I be so forward with him that

calls not on me? Well, 'tis no matter; honour pricks

me on. Yea, but how if honour prick me off when I

come on? how then? Can honour set to a leg? no: or

an arm? no: or take away the grief of a wound? no.

Honour hath no skill in surgery, then? no. What is

honour? a word. What is in that word honour? what

is that honour? air. A trim reckoning! Who hath it?

he that died o' Wednesday. Doth he feel it? no.

Doth he hear it? no. 'Tis insensible, then. Yea,

---

26.   See Appendix B for the complete scene.

to the dead. But will it not live with the living?

no. Why? detraction will not suffer it. Therefore

I'll none of it. Honour is a mere scutcheon: and so

ends my catechism.   (Act V Scene 1)

All audience members in the Globe, the Blackfriars, or at court would have caught this reference and it would have added immeasurably to their enjoyment of the scene.

TURNING

While the question-answer technique of catechizing continued in the Third Form (when the boys were about ten) we come now to a new and crucial exercise in Elizabethan schools: "turning." The Schoolmaster (or usher) would take a Latin sentence, phrase or aphorism and read it to the boys in English. The boys would render —" turn" it—into Latin to the best of their ability. Each of these Latin efforts would be compared with the Latin original, which the master would then insist they write down and memorize. The goal was to develop (by endless repetition of this technique) such knowledge of grammar and sensitivity to style that the student would eventually be able to "turn" the English immediately into the perfect Latin of the original.

The elegant Latin of the Roman playwright Terence was most often the standard against which the boys' work was measured. At Westminster, the boys started to read Terence in the Third Form. In his play *The Magnetic Lady*, Ben Jonson had a young boy say: "*Quas fecissent fabulas* ("What stories they would have made.") I understand that,

sir...I learned Terence i' the third forme at Westminster."[27]
The study of Terence introduced the use of plays as a
means of teaching boys presentation skills.

An exercise which, along with their Terence, built dramatic
expressiveness was the technique of giving the boys
short dialogues in English to turn into Latin and then
to memorize and perform. The great Spanish educator
of the early 16th century, Juan Luis Vives (1492-1540),
contemporary of Erasmus and tutor to Mary, Elizabeth
I's older half-sister, wrote an exceedingly popular book
of dialogues, in which it is apparent that he is making an
effort to relate the learning of Latin—not to great works of
classical literature, but to the boys' own familiar domestic
life.

Here is a dialogue from Vives about going to school.

> (*Cirr.* stands for *Cirrati pueri* – a boy with curled hair;
> 'cirrus' an instrument for the curling of hair.
>
> *Praet.* stands for *Praetextatus puer*, a noble or patrician boy
> whose toga was bordered with purple, worn to the age of
> 14 or 16).

Cirr.	Does it seem to you to be time to go to school?
Praet:	Certainly, it is time to go
Cirr.	I don't properly remember the way; I believe we have to go through this next street.
Praet:	How often have you already been to the school?
Cirr.	Three or four times.

---

27.   Baldwin, *Shakspere's Five-Act Structure*, 327.

Praet.	When did you first go?
Cirr:	As I think, three or four days ago.
Praet.	Well, now; isn't that enough to enable you to know the way?
Cirr.	No, not if it were a hundred times of going.
Praet.	Why, if I were to go once, never afterwards should I miss the way. But you go, against your will, and as you go, you stop and play. You don't look at the way, nor at the houses, nor any signs which would show you afterwards which way you should turn, or which way you should follow. But I observe all the points diligently, because I go gladly.

Another scene shows a boy, Tulliolus, encountering his sister and his mother as he comes home from school. Corneliona, the boy's sister, sees a paper with letters on it:

Corneliona: I say, what are those pictures? I believe they're pictures of ants. Mother, Tulliolus is bringing a lot of ants and gnats painted on a writing-tablet.

Tulliolus: Be quiet, you silly thing. They are letters...

Mother: Go and play now, my boy.

Tulliolus: I am putting my tablet and style [writing instrument] down here. If anybody disturbs them, he will be beaten by mother.

Speaking these dialogues in Latin developed a variety of oral language skills. As they practiced interchanges involving scenes of daily life the boys necessarily developed expressiveness—the dialogues were, in fact, early acting exercises.

"Turning," on the other hand, made the boys analyze linguistic expression, while encouraging grammatical correctness and nuance. As they tried to translate from one language to another, the boys increased their vocabulary, became aware of synonyms, and discovered different ways of expressing the same idea. By applying and practicing different figures of speech (simile, metaphor, *anaphora*, *epistrophe*, etc.[28]) they learned to experiment with different styles of writing and developed their imagination. The exposure to a variety of source material, and being taught to change it, gave them the sense that they were entitled to take the ideas and expressions of great authors and to "turn" them to their own use.[29]

Out of the thirty-six plays in Shakespeare's *First Folio*, five are original plot-constructions: *Titus Andronicus*, *Love's Labour's Lost*, *A Midsummer Night's Dream*, *The Merry Wives of Windsor*, and *The Tempest*. All the others are based on existing stories. In doing this, Shakespeare clearly felt at home. He, and his playwriting colleagues, had spent their school years borrowing from, and gaining praise for altering, existing sources. In this, they continued a tradition reaching back to the Middle Ages, even to the Greek tragedians. Imitation and adaptation, constantly exercised in the Tudor schoolroom, became the basis for much of the play construction of Shakespeare and his contemporaries.

---

28.   See Pogue, *Shakespeare's Figures of Speech.*
29.   See Appendix C and Appendix D.

CHAPTER 4

THE UPPER SCHOOL CURRICULUM

By the time they reached the Upper School, the young scholars had become well versed in the fundamentals of Latin grammar and vocabulary, and they were required to speak Latin in and out of school. In the Fourth, Fifth, and Sixth Forms, they would be schooled in imitation in order to have a basis for original constructions: the writing of epistles and themes; the alteration of prose into poetry (versification); and the study of rhetoric, including oratory and debate. The boys were to become eloquent, persuasive, and poetic communicators. This involved imitating classical authors, observing the rules for each discipline, and hours and hours of practice.

PATTERNING

To explore the content and form of the Elizabethan schoolboys' learning is to become increasingly aware of how carefully every subject was patterned. For instance, when the boys started Terence in the Third Form, they were taught that there were three parts to a comedy: the *protasis*, the *epitasis*, and the *catastrophe*. So familiar were these terms that both Ben Jonson and Shakespeare referred to them by name in their plays. In *Every Man Out of his Humour* (1599), Jonson wrote: "Lose not yourself, for now the *epitasis* or busy part of our subject is in act." Again in *The Magnetic Lady*: "A fine piece of logic! Do you look, Mr. Damplay, for conclusions in a *protasis*? I thought

the Law of Comedy had reserv'd that to the *catastrophe...*"
And in *King Lear,* Shakespeare had Edmund say satirically,
upon the entrance of his brother, Edgar: "Pat he comes like
the *catastrophe* of the old comedy."

When the boys started to write themes (usually based on
the *sententiae* they had learned in the lower school), they
were taught to use five parts in an argumentative form
called the *enthymeme* (a *syllogism* in which a part —the
premise or the conclusion—is unexpressed, assumed, or
taken for granted). The five parts were the proposition, the
reason, the confirmation of the reason, the embellishing,
and the conclusion. However, if a theme was based on the
rhetorical model of a complete *syllogism*, there were six
parts: the proposition, the major, the proof of the major,
the minor, the proof of the minor, and the conclusion.

When writing and presenting orations, they followed
Cicero's divisions: invention, disposition, expression,
action, and memory (sometimes translated invention,
arrangement, style, memory, and delivery). Included
in each of these disciplines was an activity called "the
embellishing," a linguistic technique of development which
required an understanding of the three "ornaments":
similitudes, examples, and apothegms.[30]

This kind of training—which forced students to make
sure that every word of writing establish, support, or
advance a structural element—would serve Shakespeare
as a playwright every time he took up his pen. Though we
may think of Shakespeare as an inspired poet, a master of
pure language, he chose to be a playwright, and successful

---

30.   Baldwin, *Shakspere's Small Latine,* 1: 333-35.

playwriting requires first and foremost the effective structuring of action.

VARYING

Equally important to the learning of structural patterns in school was the exercise of "varying," an advanced form of "turning." The boys took a phrase or sentence and worked to express the content in as many different ways as they could. First the structure of their work was to be carefully patterned; then its language was to be infinitely changeable.

For varying, the study of Johannes Susenbrotus was invaluable as he provided over 130 tropes and figures of speech to enable the boys to change their language. Many of these figures are in common use today: simile, metaphor, hyperbole, alliteration, and so forth. But Shakespeare had hours of practice with many others: *anaphora,* for instance, where each phrase began with the same word; *epistrophe,* where each phrase ended with the same word; *paranomasia*, a punning figure where words are almost identical in sound, but not in meaning; or he was set exercises in comparative techniques, such as *metalepsis* (attributing a present situation to a remote cause), or *allegoria.* While we think of allegory as a simple equivalency, Susenbrotus defined it and broke it down into nine different categories.

Allegoria included:

* *Aenigma* (riddle)

* *Paroemia* (proverb)

* *Ironia ("illusio")*

* *Sarcasmus*

* *Asteismus (urbanitas*—polite mockery)

* *Mycterismus* (to sneer)

* *Diasyrmus*   (making a ridiculous comparison to devalue an argument)

* *Antiphrasis* (the use of a word opposite to its proper meaning)

* *Charientismus* (diffusing harsh words by answering them with an appeasing mock).[31]

For varying, excerpts from Cicero and others were given to the boys to memorize and then to change or develop using the tropes of Susenbrotus. Varying was an advanced exercise in writing Latin as, in doing it, young scholars altered the Latin in the dictated phrases and sentences. Their versions were compared, each boy's with the others, and then all with the original. Varying made the boys' minds nimble, and emphasized the many different linguistic ways to express an idea.

In the Fourth Form (about age 11), the boys returned to the plays of Terence for models of good Latin speech, to the *Epistles* of Cicero for elegant letter writing, and to Aphthonius's *Progymnasmata* to deal with the challenge of oratory. With Aphthonius the boys moved decisively from studying Grammar to studying Rhetoric, as the *Progymnasmata* consisted of a set of rhetorical exercises

---

31.   http: dailytrope.com. Aug 26, 2007.

intended to prepare students for the supreme test: the creation and performance of their own orations (*gymnasmatae*).[32]

EPISTLES

Before orations, however, came practice in the writing of formal letters. Examples taken from the New Testament or from Cicero were used to analyze and imitate, as the boys prepared themselves for an activity clearly of importance in Tudor society.

Again the curriculum was organized around structure and patterning as it broke down epistles into eight different types:

suasory   (persuasive)

disuasory (persuading against)

hortatory (tending to exhort or encourage)

dehortatory   (encouraging against)

narrative (telling a tale)

gratulatory   (congratulatory)

expostulatory   (to reason earnestly, remonstrate)

commendatory   (to commend, praise)

consolatory   (to console)

---

32.   Stowe writes in detail of the curriculum for the school at Sandwich when he describes the content of Upper School classes. I assume, given the standardization of the time, that Stratford followed a very similar course content.

As it happens, an example of a Stratford schoolboy's letter has survived: a letter from the son of Shakespeare's friend Richard Quiney, written to his father, in Latin, when the boy was eleven. The year was 1598, about the time Shakespeare was writing *Henry IV Parts 1 and 2* and *Much Ado About Nothing*. Young Richard was in Stratford, his father on a business trip to London. The letter asked his father to buy two copybooks for him and his brother.[33] He thanked his father for bringing him up in religious studies (*educasti me in scrae doctrinae studiis usque ad hunc diem*) and signed himself "Thy little son most obedient to thee."[34] This small document attests to the nature of the classical education Shakespeare, like young Richard, would have received at the King Edward VI School.[35]

At the end of October 1598, Richard Quiney senior was still in London. Here he wrote the only letter still in existence addressed to William Shakespeare. Calling Shakespeare his "Dear Countryman," Quiney asked the now successful writer for a loan to cover some of the London debts Quiney had incurred as he traveled on behalf of the city. The letter seems never to have been delivered, as it was found in the Quiney papers and is kept to this day in the Birthplace Records Office in Stratford.

We actually have many examples of the epistolary skills Shakespeare practiced at school. Alan Stewart, author of *Shakespeare's Letters,* has counted 111 missives written

---

33. The request for copy books would indicate there was no place in Stratford to buy school supplies, and that these needed to come from London or another larger city.
34. Fripp, *Master Richard Quyny*, 133.
35. Ibid., 159-60. A letter to Richard Quiney from his wife (dictated to Abraham Sturley) suggests that Quiney should read Tully's (Cicero's) *Epistles*—an interesting confirmation that writers and books introduced to boys in the classroom continued to be read years after the boys had left school.

by the poet/playwright. To the regret of biographers, however, they are not longed-for personal expressions and revelations. They are couched within his work, written by innumerable, widely varied characters.

In *Twelfth Night*, for instance, Viola, disguised as Cesareo, is sent to read a commission, in the form of a letter, from Orsino to Olivia, praising her virtues. The most famous, perhaps, of Shakespeare's letters appears in the same play. In Act II Scene 5, Malvolio discovers and reads aloud the letter Maria has written to entrap him and which sends him—in his ludicrous yellow, cross-gartered stockings— to please the woman who, the letter has led him to believe, is in love with him.

Macbeth's letter to his wife, inspiring her determination to kill Duncan, is unforgettable, as is Phebe's cruel letter to her pathetic swain, Sylvius, in *As You Like It* (an interesting piece of evidence that country maids of the time were sometimes literate and their male followers sometimes not). Alan Stewart notes that only five of the 36 plays lack letters, while the forward movement of the plot of *King Lear* absolutely depends upon them.

When we look for Shakespeare's own voice, we find only two more or less conventional pleas for patronage, addressed to the Earl of Southampton, written to appear before his epic poems, *Venus and Adonis* and *The Rape of Lucrece*.

It could be argued, however, that many if not most of his 154 Sonnets were highly personal letters. He wrote the majority to a dazzling young man; some to the famous

Dark Lady; and one, #145, containing a pun ("hate away" "Hathaway") that connected Shakespeare to his wife. As these poems were all written in strict sonnet form, Shakespeare combined in them his school day training in letter writing with that other crucial upper school exercise: versification.

VERSIFYING

In the Upper School at Winchester, the boys memorized twelve lines of Ovid a week, or about 500 lines a year. In addition, John Sturm in his *System of Education* advised that "In Cicero and Virgil the boys should memorize at least the things useful for imitation, and probably all. They should memorize something every day just to exercise the memory itself. There should be regular and frequent repetitions."[36] In repeating their Ovid, Fifth Form boys taught the Fourth Formers and thus reviewed their past verses, plus learning 500 lines more. Sixth and Seventh Formers continued the exercise, so as they reached adulthood, two thousand or more lines of one of Latin's greatest poets—and the habit of memorization—were fixed in Elizabethan schoolboys' minds.[37]

Ovid was studied everywhere. He was Shakespeare's favorite poet—a preference shared by many of his contemporaries (both writers and audience members). In his *Metamorphoses,* Ovid retold the ancient Greek and Roman myths, and his work was filled with imagination, sensuality, and lyricism. References to Ovid crop up incidentally throughout Shakespeare's work; in *Venus and Adonis* and in the Pyramus and Thisbe play in *A Midsummer*

---

36.   Baldwin, *Shakspere's Small Latine,* 1: 287.
37.   Ibid., 160.

Night's Dream, the borrowing was direct and revelatory. By comparing the original with Shakespeare's result, we can experience the thrill of watching his writer's mind at work (see Appendix D).

In the Fifth Form, the master would also read to the boys from the *Eclogues* of Virgil (or, according to the school statutes in Sandwich, "some chaste poet") and in doing so introduced them to the rules of versification. If he needed help or advice in how to teach his young charges to change a subject from prose into verse, the master could turn to John Brinsley's chapter in *The Grammar Schoole* entitled "Versifying: The most plain way how to enter to make a verse without bodging."[38]

Imagine you are a Latin teacher today wanting to experiment with your students by teaching them how Shakespeare learned to write poetry. Brinsley is here to help. Speaking of the students, he advises the teacher:

1. To look that they be able in manner to write true Latin, and a good phrase in prose, before they begin to meddle with making a verse.

2. That they have read some poetry first... viz, Ovid's *de Tristibus*, or *de Ponto*, some piece of his *Metamorphoses* or of Virgil, and be well acquainted with their Poetical phrases.

3. I find this a most easy and pleasant way to enter them; that for all the first books of Poetry... they use to read them daily out of the Grammatical translations: first resolving every verse into the Grammatical order, like as it is in the translation... For the making of a verse is nothing but the turning of words forth of the

---

38.   "Bodging" is a word related to "botching."

Grammatical order, into the Rhetorical, in some kind of meter, which we call verse...

4. Then... that they be made very cunning in the rules of versifying, so as to be able to give you readily each rule...[39]

Brinsley concluded by saying, "Lastly in this exercise as in all the rest, I hold daily practice and diligence (following the best patterns) to be the surest and speediest guide; and which will bring in time much perfection, where there is aptness of nature concurring."[40]

Shakespeare gave a nod to the ubiquitous verse making of the era in *Love's Labour's Lost,* where he had each of the young lovers write his lady a sonnet (giving Shakespeare the challenge of writing four different sonnets in four different voices—varying with a vengeance).

If Shakespeare himself had a talent for verse, he knew others did not always share it. He indicated his sympathy with them in *Much Ado About Nothing,* where Benedick gives up trying to craft a poem for Beatrice. Benedick claims he cannot show his love in verse, though he's tried: "I can find out no rhyme to 'lady' but 'baby,' an innocent rhyme," he says; " for 'scorn', 'horn,' a hard rhyme; for 'school', 'fool,' a babbling rhyme" and concludes despairingly: "I was not born under a rhyming planet..." (Act V Scene 2)

Brinsley, however, noted three aspects of training in versification which related to writing for the theatre:

---

39.   Brinsley, *The Grammar School,* 193-95. See Appendix A for a continuation of Brinsley's instructions.
40.   Ibid.

"Cause also so many as you would have to learn together..." said Brinsley, an idea he expanded upon in his book. He encouraged collaborative writing, which dominated the world of the playwright in London. After working with groups in school, playwrights would have found it natural to accept the influence of others. This is not to say Shakespeare's plays were primarily written in collaboration with other writers, but that an individual who had gone through Brinsley's process in an English grammar school in the sixteenth century would have been accustomed to the challenges and benefits of working in concert with others.

Brinsley then added: "... cause them [the students] to contrast their lectures, drawing seven or eight verses into four or five, or fewer; yet still laboring to express the whole matter of their Author in their own verse..." Here we discover that the intense and often difficult-to-decipher concentration of ideas and images in some of Shakespeare's writing was taught, practiced, and prized in school. Finally, we see that students wrote their ideas in prose first, then versified them. There is an anecdote that claims that after seeing *Henry IV Parts 1* and *2*, Queen Elizabeth asked Shakespeare to write a comedy showing "the fat knight in love." Shakespeare began writing *The Merry Wives of Windsor* in response to this request, and completed it in two weeks. The play is almost entirely in prose, suggesting that Shakespeare simply didn't have time to versify it.

Shakespeare, unlike his Benedick, *was* born under a rhyming planet. He could versify anything. But, as important as it was, the art of versifying was not the acme of effective writing. It was just an alternative linguistic form. The heart of thrilling communication lay in the power to move—in a word, rhetoric—the study of which was the focus of Shakespeare's last years in school.

RHETORIC

In the Fifth Form, the students continued the formal study of rhetoric they began in the Fourth. In addition to writing orations, they took part in extemporaneous disputations to practice their growing rhetorical skill.

Rhetoric was training in argumentation. It involved the structure of action, intention, and language in such a way as to arouse feeling and to succeed in persuasion. It is inherently dramatic as one person on the side of an argument tries to change the mind, or affect the emotions, of another.

Classical rhetoric was expressed through the use of both linguistic and structural devices. For the latter, the boys studied the *Rhetorica Ad Herennium* (at the time attributed to Cicero, though now thought to be of unknown authorship), which was historically the very first book of Latin rhetoric. It dated from the 90s BC, and was still used to guide students in Shakespeare's day. As in other disciplines, a key was the breaking down of rhetoric into component parts.

The speaker needed to possess the faculties of Invention, Arrangement, Style, Memory, and Delivery, defined in the *Ad Herennium* as follows:

Invention is the devising of matter, true or plausible, that would make the case convincing.

Arrangement is the ordering and distribution of the matter, making clear the place to which each thing is to be assigned.

Style is the adaptation of suitable words and sentences to the matter devised.

Memory is the firm retention in the mind of the matter, words, and arrangement.

Delivery is the graceful regulation of voice, countenance, and gesture.

Invention and arrangement, the first faculties, involved conceiving and writing the text. For this, there were again five steps:

Exordium: in which the writer is to gain attention by using anecdotes, quotes, or analogies to capture attention and then connects them to the specific topic.

Narratio: in which the author sets out the argument, thesis or point to be proven.

Divisio: an outline of the main points, to clarify what comes next.

Confirmatio: supporting points, and or evidence (often three) for the thesis.

Confutatio: setting out and refutation of the opposing arguments.

Conclusio: a summary of the argument, describing the urgency of the viewpoint and the actions that could be taken.

If these did not give the boys enough to work with, an equally influential treatise on rhetoric, Cicero's *Topics*,[41] listed sixteen forms of arguments such as Definition, Contraries, Similarity, and so forth,[42] while Susenbrotus and his tropes were always to hand.

Leslie O'Dell, in *Shakespearean Language*, discusses in detail Shakespeare's figures of speech and rhetoric. From her we'll borrow a few examples of patterns the boys utilized when writing orations.[43] The first are structural:

Apoplanesis: digressing to another topic in order to avoid the issue.

Aporia: doubting or deliberating with oneself.

Anthypophora: reasoning with oneself, asking questions and answering.

Concessio: granting a point.

Orcos: taking an oath to swear one speaks the truth.

Paromologia: admitting something that does not favor one's argument and then introducing a point that refutes what has just been granted.

---

41.   //www.classicpersuasion.org/pw/cicero/cicero-topics.htm
42.   Leslie O'Dell further explains and defines these topics in *Shakespearean Language*, 158.
43.   O'Dell, 167-68.

The next are linguistic:

Alliteration: repetition of consonant sounds.

Anaphora: beginning a series of clauses with the same word or words.

Antithesis: placing contraries in opposition.

Definition: explaining the nature or essence of a subject.

Epimone: repetition of the same point in the same words.

Syncresis: comparing contrasting things in contrasting clauses.

Systrophe: listing many definitions of one thing.

Observe how Shakespeare uses them, and those from the *Ad Herrenium,* in this speech of Benedick's (*Much Ado About Nothing*, Act II Scene 3). Structural elements of structure are bolded to distinguish them from the linguistic elements, or figures of speech.

BENEDICK

I do much wonder that one man, seeing how much	*(exordium)*
another man is a fool when he dedicates his	
behaviors to love, will, after he hath laughed at	
such shallow follies in others, become the argument	
of his own scorn by failing in love: and such a man	*(definition)*
is Claudio.	
I have known when there was no music	*(narratio)*
with him but the drum and the fife;	

and now had he   *(antithesis)*
rather hear the tabour and the pipe:
I have known when he would have walked   **(divisio)**
ten mile a-foot to see a good armour;
(syncresis)
and now will he lie ten nights awake
carving the fashion of a new doublet.

He was wont to   **(divisio)**
speak plain and to the purpose, like an honest man   *(alliteration)*
and a soldier; and now is he turned orthography; his   *(antithesis)*
words are a very fantastical banquet, just so many   **(confirmatio)**
strange dishes.

May I be so converted and see with these eyes?   **(aporia)**
I cannot tell; I think not:

I will not be sworn, but love   **(concession)**
may transform me to an oyster; but   **(confutation)**
I'll take my oath on it, till he have made an oyster   **(orcos)**
of me, he shall never make me such a fool.

One woman is fair, yet I am well;   **(commoratio)**
another is wise, yet I am well;   **(confutatio)**
another virtuous, yet I am well;   *(epimone)*
but till all graces be in one woman,
one woman shall not come in my grace.

Rich she shall be, that's certain;   **(apoplanesis)**
wise, or I'll none;
(systrophe)
virtuous, or I'll never cheapen her   ;   *(anaphora)*
fair, or I'll never look on her;
mild, or come not near me;   *(antithesis)*
noble, or not I for an angel;
of good discourse,
an excellent musician,
and her hair shall be of what colour it please God.

There is not enough room to indicate all the linguistic devices Shakespeare has incorporated in this speech. He wrote it in 1597-98, when he was thirty-four years old and at the peak of his rhetorical ability. *Julius Caesar* and *Henry V* were written at the same time and explode with extraordinary public and private argument. Who knows if, twenty years after leaving school, Shakespeare even remembered the name for each device he used— quite probably he did not. But he had practiced them in the classroom until they filled his mind and waited "like greyhounds in the slip" to energize and shape his language.

The boys added Sallust, another Roman historian, to their reading of Cicero, and with these examples in mind, turned to Aphthonius and his *Progymnasmata* (detailed in Chapter 7) to begin their own efforts in writing orations.

The study of rhetoric—this power to move—is evident not only in the speeches in Shakespeare's plays, but in the structure of the plays themselves. They reflect yet one more important pattern, this time from Aristotle: *Ethos, Pathos, Logos.*

Ethos refers in part to the skill of the orator in connecting with his audience and establishing his authority. For example, in the Forum scene in *Julius Caesar,* both Brutus and Mark Antony claim to be the friend of Caesar—each seeks in this way to establish his credibility before the hostile crowd. *Pathos* on the other hand focuses on appeals to emotion, often achieved by stimulating the imagination by referring to a moving experience on the part of the speaker, which he shares with the audience. And finally,

Logos entails appeals to Logic involving principles of deductive and inductive reasoning.

An important part of the study of rhetoric was effective presentation. Fourth Form through Sixth Form students continued the tradition of acting Latin classical plays—in a number of schools, children acted scenes from Terence and Plautus on a weekly basis. "Thus," says Samuel Schoenbaum, "was Shakespeare introduced to classical comedy and the five-act structure of plays."[44]

But Shakespeare learned not just techniques of construction, but how to speak lines. Thomas Jenkins, his schoolmaster, knew that at Merchant Taylors', where many of his Oxford classmates had received their grammar-school education,

> (Richard Mulcaster) always kept the spoken word in the forefront of his mind when he taught Latin. When he expounded the mysteries of punctuation to his classes he did it as a singing teacher might, with the emphasis on 'tunable uttering.' A parenthesis meant the use of a lower and quicker voice, a comma was a place to catch the breath a little, and a period was a place where the breath could be caught completely. This sort of training would have been of great use to William Shakespeare when he started work as a professional actor.[45]

Lastly, in the Sixth Form (ages 12-13), the boys embarked on the study of Greek.[46] Although less practical than Latin, Greek was studied in order that students could read the

---

44.   Schoenbaum, *William Shakespeare: A Compact Documentary Life*, 69.
45.   Chute, 17. Lynn Enterline, in *Shakespeare's Schoolroom*, heightens our awareness of the extent to which Tudor education focused on performance, not just vocal but gestural as well.
46.   In some schools, Greek began in the Fifth Form. This seems to have been the choice of the Schoolmaster.

New Testament in its original language. Shakespeare would have studied at least a bit of Greek (had he not, Ben Jonson would have credited him with none at all—rather than accusing him of having "less" of it). As Greek was not usually introduced into the curriculum until the Sixth Form, Shakespeare's knowing some is a powerful argument for his having stayed in school, despite his father's financial reversals.[47] Thomas Jenkins, the schoolmaster, had become proficient in Greek at St. John's College, Oxford, as that was a focus of that college's curriculum. There is no reason to suspect that he would not have included it as one of the courses for the boys in the Upper Forms at the King Edward VI School in Stratford.

---

47.   In some of the larger, more sophisticated schools, Hebrew was also introduced at this time but that was not likely in Stratford, where serious young scholars, and teachers trained in Hebrew were rare.

CHAPTER 5

SHAKESPEARE'S SCHOOLBOOKS

For poor students at some disadvantaged schools, books were not easily available. For them, instruction was by dictation, response, and repetition—a highly active aural and oral experience. Schools acquired Latin dictionaries, other reference books, and perhaps even a collection of textbooks, by purchase and donation. The most valuable reference books at a school were chained to a shelf. Vicar John Bretchgirdle, who had baptized Shakespeare, left his copy of Sir Thomas Elyot's Latin-English dictionary, *Biblioteca Elkotae*, to the King Edward VI School.[48] In a small school like Stratford's, one would think it possible to collect the necessary books and assign them to the boys as needed from year to year.[49]

But in many, if not most, cases, children were expected to own books and bring them to school. At St. Paul's, the rules for parents wanting to enroll their children said: "you shall find him convenient books to his learning." While in Lichfield, "six poor pupils, selected from the children of the poor men in Lichfield were to receive 1 pound, 6s 8d each for the purchase of books and brooms with which to sweep the school..."[50] Robert Pursglove spent nine years at St. Paul's, then went on to found two schools: Tideswell

---

48.   Honan, 44.
49.   This is how textbooks were handled in 20th century elementary schools in America. When my husband went to elementary school in southern Illinois in the late 1940s, as he wrote his name in the book he'd been given, he found his own mother's name written high on the list of names above his. The book had been passed down from class to class for 30 years.
50.   Stowe, 126.

in Derbyshire in 1560 and Guisborough[51] in York in 1561. Pursglove said, "And no scholars shall be suffered to continue in the said school over one month except he have books necessary for his form or else daily write his lessons with his own hand."[52] Baldwin speculated that unless books were distributed at the school in Stratford, Shakespeare would have had new books. His father, brought up on a farm some four miles outside of Stratford, did not have the opportunity to go to school, and therefore would not have had books to pass on to his oldest son.[53]

An investment in schoolbooks paid off as the family grew. In Shakespeare's family, the texts bought for William would have been used when his three younger brothers went to school. Texts changed so slowly that it is probable Shakespeare's son, Hamnet, took William Shakespeare's books with him in his satchel when he went off to school twenty years after his father.

---

51.   Ibid., 43. Stowe reports: "In Guisborough the corporation was to consist of two wardens, one school-master, and twelve poor persons... six of each sex, the women to be at least sixty-three years of age and to have been inhabitants of Guisborough for at least three years..." This is an intriguing structure for a school organization and makes one want to know more about Robert Pursglove, the school, and the elderly women of Guisborough.

52.   Baldwin, *Shakspere's Smalle Latin* 1:439; modern spelling mine.

53.   Ibid., 494. The extent of John Shakespeare's education remains a point of contention among scholars. He signed with a mark rather than a signature and seems to have had little formal schooling. For two year-long terms, however, he was Chamberlain of the Stratford Corporation, the official treasurer of the town, which argues—as do his years of service on the Corporation, including a year as bailiff—for intelligence and training. He could well have been able to read but not write, as writing was often done by scribes and not felt to be a requirement for a middle-class citizen (similar to the attitude that mid-20th century businessmen did not need to know how to type because there were secretaries to do that for them). Scholars seem to be in accord that a man of John Shakespeare's ambition would have seen that his son was educated to the standards of the day, which meant William would have been enrolled in the local grammar school, certainly the premise of this book.

School books of the time fell into four categories: recent texts specifically written to instruct students or to guide their teachers; writings of great authors of the classical past in the form of complete books or collections of excerpts; writings of respected authors of the modern era; and religious texts. They could also be divided into books in prose and books in verse, or books in Latin (most) versus books in English (the religious texts).

Textbooks written especially for children began with *The Horn Book,* followed by the *Primer* (a collection of private devotions),[54] the *Absey,* and the *Short Catechism.* The *King's Primer* of 1545 included "English translations of the daily hours: Matins, Lauds, Prime, Terce, Sext, None, Vespers and Compline, translations of the Apostles' Creed and Lord's Prayer, and various private prayers in English."[55]

In the first years of grammar school, Lily's *Latin Grammar* was the earliest and most ubiquitous Latin text, followed by Leonard Culman's *Sententiae Pueriles* (collected for teachers in Brinsley's *Ludus Literarius: or, The Grammar Schoole*), and Corderius's *Colloquies.* The most widely used Greek texts were Cleonard's *Greek Grammar* and *St. John's Gospel.*

Cato and Aesop were the first classical writers read by students since the *Maxims* of the first and the *Fables* of the second were particularly suitable for youngsters. Ovid,

54.   *A Short Catechism...for All Schoolmasters to Teach* by John Ponet, Bishop of Winchester, was printed with versions of the Articles from 1553, and Alexander Nowell's two forms of 1570 and 1572 likewise met the need for a longer catechism than the *Prayer Book* provided. http://mb-soft.com/believe/txw/catechis.htm. This is a different publication from Luther's famous Catechism published early in the 16th century.

55.   Long, 27.

Cicero, Virgil, Terence, Horace, Plautus, Juvenal, Persius, Seneca, and Aphthonius followed, with Livy, Sallust, and Suetonius possibly studied as well. The boys also read in Latin many of the great writers of the Renaissance, including Erasmus, Mantuan, Susenbrotus, and Palingenius. Through these books, Shakespeare and his schoolmates absorbed an astonishing amount of classical literature and history during their years in grammar school.

Although Latin ruled, English was not ignored. The boys were referred constantly to the Geneva *Bible* (including the books in the *Apocrypha*) and the *Book of Common Prayer* (which included the *Catechism*). Long observes: "The Reformation *Bible* and Cranmer's *Book of Common Prayer* have remained the two supreme glories of English religious literature... There is no doubt that the repetition of their beautiful and smoothly flowing phrases day by day and week by week had a profound and ennobling influence on the development of English language and thought..."[56]

The religious books meant that, for school-aged boys, Sundays were not a day of rest. They had to take note of the sermons or homilies in order to answer questions about them on Monday at school. They chanted the *Psalms* of Buchanan or sang the metered *Psalms* of Sternhold and Hopkins as part of Sunday services.

Here are the first two verses of Psalm 112, from the Geneva *Bible*:

> Praise ye the Lord. Blessed is the man, that feareth the Lord, and delighteth greatly in his commandments.

---

56.   Ibid., 26.

His seed shall be mighty upon earth: the generation of the righteous shall be blessed.

As versified by Sternhold and Hopkins, two rewriters of the *Psalms*, they become:

The man is blest that God doth fear,

And that his laws doth love indeed:

His seed on earth God will uprear,

And bless such as from him proceed.

References to the *Bible*, the *Book of Common Prayer*, and the *Psalms* are common in Shakespeare's work.[57] When King Henry V seeks to express his gratitude after the English victory at Agincourt in *Henry V* (Act IV Scene 8), he calls out to his men: "Let there be sung '*Non Nobis'* and '*Te Deum.*'" The ceremonial exit from that scene is thus accompanied by the full cast singing two of the great psalms of praise and thanks, perhaps as versified by Sternhold and Hopkins or straight from the *Book of Common Prayer.*

---

57.   See Noble, *Shakespeare's Biblical Knowledge,* and Marx, *Shakespeare and the Bible,* among others.

CHAPTER 6

SCHOOLBOOKS IN THE LOWER FORMS

For a more detailed look at the schoolbooks, when and how they were used, we turn to Charles Hoole's *A New Discovery of the Old Art of Teaching Schoole,* published in 1636. Though his book came out 75 years after Shakespeare went to school, Hoole's view was to the past and traditions changed slowly. He began by explaining:

The custom was to enter boys to the School one by one, as they were fit for the *Accidence* and to let them proceed therein severally, till so many others came to them, as were fit to be ranked with them in a form. These were first put to read the *Accidence,* and afterwards made to commit it to memory; which when they had done, they were exercised in construing and parsing the examples in the English Rules, and this was called the first form... [58]

So the First Form began with Lily's *Accidence*. Other books followed. (Hoole's descriptive list of readings precedes each Form's discussion.)

FIRST FORM

Lily's Latin Grammar, the Accidence, *Sententiae Pueriles, Pueriles Confabulationes,* Aesop's Fables, Cato's *Maxims,* the *Primer* (including the Short Catechism), and *A Book of Private Prayer.*

---

58.   Baynes, *What Shakespeare Learnt at School* http:// www.shakespeareonline. com/biography/whatdidshkread.html. I have updated the spelling.

The technical title of the universally used *Latin Grammar* was Lily's *A Short Introduction to Grammar Generally to be Used* or *The Queen's Grammar, with the Accidence*. The book had two parts, the *Shorte Introduction* (the part also called the *Accidence*), and the grammar proper, or *Brevissima Institutio*, informally called Lily's *Latin Grammar*.[59]

Marchette Chute observes,

> Lily was the first head-master of the school at St. Paul's Cathedral, and his book must have made him more cordially hated by harassed seven-year-olds than any man before or since. The whole of the English educational system united to pound Lily's Latin grammar into the heads of the young, and if a schoolboy was wise he resigned himself to having to memorize the whole book.[60]

Though the title is in English, the text itself is almost completely Latin, and is organized around how to manipulate properly the eight Latin parts of speech. A long chapter is given to each.

Shakespeare's knowledge of Lily is everywhere observable in his plays, from the earliest to the latest. In the second scene of Act IV of *Titus Andronicus*, Titus sends a bundle of weapons to Demetrius and Chiron with a scroll on which are written two lines of Horace:

> DEMETRIUS: What's here? a scroll, and written round about. Let's see.
>
> *(Reads) Integer vitae, scelerisque purus, Non eget Mauri jaculis, nec arcu.*
>
> ["The man who is upright and free of vice,

---

59.   Lily is variously spelled Lyly or Lilly.
60.   Chute, 15.

Needs not Moorish spears or the bow."]

CHIRON: O, 'tis a verse in Horace, I know it well, I read it in the grammar long ago.

AARON: Ay, just – a verse in Horace, right, you have it.

The verse Chiron alludes to is a familiar memorized quotation from Lily.[61]

In *Richard III*, Queen Margaret ends an embittered speech with:

MARGARET: Who sues to thee and cries 'God save the queen'?

Where be the bending peers that flatter'd thee?

Where be the thronging troops that followe'd thee?

Decline all this, and see what now thou art.

Richard III Act IV scene 4

In this selection we may see or hear the word "decline" and think "refuse." Shakespeare's audience readily heard it as a metaphor for a grammatical construct—"decline"—as in inflect or change the endings of a Latin noun to alter the meaning and express different levels of reality.

Much later, toward the end of his career, Shakespeare is still alluding to Lily when in *Antony and Cleopatra* Antony says of Caesar:

---

61.   http://www.oxfordShakespeare.com/OxfordAsShakespeare/EssayOxford AsShakesp.pdf

ANTONY: I dare him therefore

To lay his gay comparisons apart,

And answer me declined, sword against sword.

Antony and Cleopatra Act III scene 13

In his lengthy chapter on Shakespeare's grammar, Baldwin says, "... here there may be a figure that Antony shall be 'declined' grammatically from the 'comparative' superiority he now holds through fortune to the 'positive' degree of sword to sword unaided."[62] Often the lines we struggle with in Shakespeare, or ones where we miss a double meaning, are difficult precisely because we no longer share the academic traditions and vocabulary he alludes to instinctively.

From *Titus Andronicus* (c.1590) to *Love's Labour's Lost* (c.1592) to *Richard III* (c.1593) to *The Merry Wives of Windsor* (1598) to *Antony and Cleopatra* (1606-07), and in most of the plays before and after, Shakespeare's thought patterns turned again and again to his, and his contemporaries', ingrained memory of Lily's *Latin Grammar.*[63]

After the *Accidence*, the boys turned to *Sententiae Pueriles*, the simple, moralistic phrases and sentences collected in pamphlet-style leaflets for the boys to translate from English to Latin and Latin to English. These greatly influenced the boys in forming the sentence patterns and idioms of Elizabethan English.

---

62.   Baldwin, *Shakspere's Small Latine*, 1:568.
63.   For Shakespeare's examples of the teaching of Lily in his youth, see Appendix A.

Cato's *Maxims* were similarly used. A 2nd century BC Roman historian, Cato was the first to write and publish in prose. Though his only complete work is *De Agricultura,* he was a gifted writer of aphorisms, which continued in a more sophisticated way the work that the younger boys began in the *Sententiae Pueriles.* Here are some *Maxims* Cato wrote to his son:

> "An angry man opens his mouth and shuts his eyes."

> "If you are ruled by mind you are a king; if by body, a slave.

> "Speech is the gift of all, but thought of the few."

> "I think the first virtue is to restrain the tongue; he approaches nearest the gods who knows how to be silent, even though he is in the right."[64]

Aesop's *Fables* and a good manual of school conversation, such as the *Pueriles Confabulationes,* came next.

Shakespeare alluded often to Aesop in his plays. At least three times he referred to one fable, "The Countryman and a Snake." In this, Aesop told of a countryman who saw a snake nearly frozen to death. Out of pity he took the snake home, fed him, and warmed him by the fire. As soon as the snake recovered, he attacked the man and his family.

And so, aptly, in *Henry VI Part 2* Act III, York warned:

> I fear me you but warm the starved snake,

> Who, cherish'd in your breasts, will sting your hearts.

---

64.   http://thinkexist.com/quotes/cato_the_elder/

In turn, Richard II cried out against his enemies (*Richard II A*ct III Scene 2), calling them "villains, vipers, damn'd without redemption! .... Snakes, in my heart-blood warm'd that sting my heart!"

And in the same play, York brought the image back one more time:

> Forget to pity him, lest thy pity prove
>
> A serpent that will sting thee to the heart.

> (*Richard II* Act V Scene 3)

Aesop told of a fox who wanted some delicious grapes, but called them sour when he couldn't get to them. Shakespeare alluded to this fable in Act II Scene 1 of *All's Well That Ends Well,* when Lafeu asked: "O, will you eat no grapes, my royal fox?" And in *King Lear* Shakespeare made reference to the feckless grasshopper and the industrious ant in "The Ant and the Grasshopper," when Kent said to Lear:

> "We'll set thee to school to an ant to teach thee there's no labouring i' the winter." (Act II Scene 4)

Everyone educated in the Tudor system knew Aesop. In a pamphlet of 1592, a jealous colleague, Robert Greene, disparaged Shakespeare, calling him "an upstart crow,"[65] referring to Aesop's "The Crow and the Borrowed Feathers."

This fable criticized people who claimed they owned something they in fact did not possess. A crow, said Aesop, perceived she was plain and ugly. She expressed her grievances to an eagle and the eagle suggested she

---

65. See Anders for many more examples.

borrow feathers from other, more colorful birds. The crow got feathers from the peacock, the dove, and more. When she thought she was beautiful enough she began to jeer at the other birds. The ones who had loaned her feathers complained to the eagle, who answered: Each one of you take back your feathers, and you will leave the crow humiliated and ashamed. The birds took back their feathers and the crow found herself naked and ugly.

Greene was accusing Shakespeare of borrowing the "feathers" of the university-educated playwrights, and wanted to expose him as a fraud. Shakespeare's friends came to his defense, but all knew Greene had found an image from Aesop that every reader would recognize, and therefore one that would hurt.[66]

SECOND FORM

> Continue Lily and the *Sententiae Pueriles*, the Catechism, Aesop, Cato, the *Pueriles Confabulatiunculae*, and Corderius's *Colloquies*

In describing the Second Form routines, Hoole emphasized the importance of repetition:

> The second form was to repeat the Accidents for Parts; to say fore-noons Lessons in Propria quae maribus, Quae genus, and as in praesenti, which they repeated memoriter, construed and parsed; to say an after-noon's lessone in Sententiae Pueriles, which they repeated by heart, and construed and parsed; they repeated their tasks every Friday memoriter, and parsed their Sentences out of the English.

---

66.   In *Shakspere's Small Latine* vol. 1, Chapter 1, Baldwin goes into minute detail on source material and references concerning Aesop.

Hoole's words illustrate how, during Shakespeare's day, writers moved back and forth from English to Latin in the same phrase, sentence, or paragraph. This can be noted in other documents of the time – wills, inventories, lawsuits. The language of learning was gradually shifting from Latin to English, but it would be the twentieth century before Latin finally loosened its grip.

Pueriles Confabulatiunculae is the same title for two books of conversations: one by John Brinsley in 1617, and another by Joseph Webbe in 1627. Although both editions postdated Shakespeare's grammar school days, they represented a popular way of teaching colloquial Latin. Like Vives, whose dialogues were quoted earlier, these men chose the most mundane of subjects. Webbe, who subtitled his book *Childrens talke*, started with the humorously universal problem of getting a boy to wake up in the morning. You can well imagine how the boys enjoyed acting out the following dialogue in Latin.

Recognizing that the Second Form boys were still early linguists, the English sentences were first arranged down the left side of the page while the Latin translation was to the right, as in the following example from Webbe:

(Modernized spelling):

Mother and Joseph

Son Joseph,	Josephe fili,	(Mother speaking)
son;	mi fili;	
Why Joseph.	mi Josephe.	

| What would you? | Quid vis? | (Joseph speaking) |
| 'Tis time to rise. | Est tempus surgendi. | (M.) |

I beseech you-- let me rest yet a little while.	Sine me, obsecro adhuc pan- lulum requiescere.	(J.)
You have slept enough. Arise my son.	Dormistum est satis. Surge, mi fili.	(M.)
How many hours have I slept?	Quot horas dormiui?	(J.)
Almost ten, too long.	Ferme decem, nimium diu.	(M.)
I would I might sleep my fill.	Utinam liceat ad sa- sietatem dormire.	(J.)
Do but open thy eyes.	Aperitantum oculos.	(M.)
In sooth, I cannot.	Non possum herclei.	(J.)
See what fine weather 'tis abroad.	Cerne quam sudum est saris.	(M.)

The most popular writer of these dialogues in Shakespeare's day was the eminent scholar and teacher Corderius. His *Colloquies* contained one hundred little dialogues, presented only in Latin, and therefore intended for boys who had mastered enough of the language to figure them out without translation. The first Corderius dialogue, in fact, concerned two boys chatting about practicing their Latin speech.

Corderius, like Vives in an earlier day, illustrated the colloquial, conversational use of Latin, which was so essential a feature of grammar school discipline in the 16th and 17th centuries.[67]

THIRD FORM

Continue with *Lily* and the *Testament, Aesop* and *Cato;* add Castellio's *Dialogues,* Mantuan's *Eclogues,* and Helvicus's *Colloquies,* plus Palingenius's *Zodiacus Vitae* and possibly Terence.

Hoole continued:

The third form was enjoined first to repeat two parts together every morning, one out of the *Accidents* and the other out of that forementioned part of the *Grammar,*... their forenoons lessons were two days in Aesop's *Fables,* and other two days in Cato; both which they construed and parsed, and said Cato *memoriter;* these Lessons they translated into English, and repeated all on Fridays, construing out of the Translations into Latin.

In the Third Form the students continued with Cato, whose influence on the growth of Latin literature was immense. He was the author of *Origines,* the first history of Rome composed in Latin. This work, of whose seven books only a few fragments survive, related the traditions of the founding of Rome and other Italian cities. Reading this Roman history must have made the ancient Greeks

---

67.   In his article about the translation of the King James *Bible* ("The Bible of King James," *National Geographic,* December 2011), Adam Nicolson expresses surprise that the translators had their editorial discussions "extraordinarily, mostly in Latin and partly in Greek" (45). This was in the early 17th century when such conversations would have been the norm among scholars—speaking Latin (and, at the university level, Greek) was what they had all been trained to do.

and Romans intensely real to a boy of Shakespeare's imagination.

Other books in use in the Third Form were written by Renaissance authors writing in Latin. They include more *Dialogues*, those of Castellio, an early follower of Calvin who later became one of his great critics. Early in his career, as an exercise for teaching Latin, Castellio reworked the *Old* and *New Testament* into a dialogue in Latin and French. This small book was widely read throughout Europe and had over forty editions.[68]

Because virtually everything that was studied in the Middle Ages and in the Renaissance was written in Latin, writers from all over Europe were known universally—Castellio, born in French-speaking Savoi; Vives, born in Spain; Mantuan, born in Italy; all became accessible to English schoolboys as they acquired the common language: Latin.

Mantuanus, whose *Eclogues* the boys studied, was a late fifteenth century Italian humanist and prolific writer of both prose and verse. We know Shakespeare was acquainted with Mantuan (the English version of his name) from the sentimental reference to him in Shakespeare's early, intellectual comedy *Love's Labour's Lost* (Act IV Scene 2):

HOLOFERNES:

Fauste, precor gelida quando pecus omne sub umbra

Ruminat,--

---

68.   Hillar.www.socinian.org/castellio.html

["Faustus, I pray that while the entire flock ruminates under the shade –"]

and so forth. Ah, good old Mantuan! I

may speak of thee as the traveller doth of Venice;

Venetia, Venetia,

Chi non ti vede non ti pretia.

Old Mantuan, old Mantuan! who understandeth thee

not, loves thee not.

The poet Michael Drayton was a contemporary of Shakespeare and affirmed what schoolboys read at the time—and at what age:

And when that once *Pueriles* I had read,

And newly had my *Cato* construed,

In my small selfe I greatly marveil'd then,

Amongst all other, what strange kind of men

These Poets were; And pleased with the name,

To my milde Tutor merrily I came,

(For I was then a proper goodly page,

Much like a Pigmy, scarce ten yeares of age)

Clasping my slender armes about his thigh.

O my deare master! Cannot you (quoth I)

Make me a Poet...

When shortly he began

And first read to me honest *Mantuan*...[69]

Brought up as a page in the household of Sir Henry Goodere of Poleworth, Drayton received his education from a tutor. His poem shows that he studied the same writers as boys covered in the schools. Though Drayton and Shakespeare were both known as Warwickshire lads, they came from opposite parts of the county. This changed when Anne Goodere, the daughter of Drayton's patron—a girl with whom Drayton had had the misfortune to fall in love—married Sir Henry Rainsford and came to live at Clifford Chambers, a town just two miles from Stratford. Drayton visited the Rainsfords frequently for the rest of their lives and perhaps spent time with Shakespeare. John Ward, the Vicar of Stratford's church in 1662, gathering information about Shakespeare nearly fifty years after Shakespeare had died, passed on an anecdote that he had heard concerning the circumstances of Shakespeare's death. "Shakespeare, Drayton, and Ben Jonson," he wrote, "had a merry meeting, and it seems drank too hard, for Shakespeare died of a feavour there contracted."

There is no corroboration of this story, but in 1627, Drayton evaluated his great contemporary in an epistle to Henry Reynolds:

And be it said of thee,

Shakespeare, thou hadst as smooth a Comicke vaine,

Fitting the socke,[70] and in thy natural braine,

---

69.   Baldwin, *Shakspere's Small Latine and Lesse Greeke*, 1: 644.
70.   McDonald, 100: "A reference to the slipper worn by the classical actor of comedy."

> As strong conception, and as Cleere a rage,
>
> As any one that trafiqu'd with the stage.[71]

Drayton had also "trafiqu'd with the stage," writing plays for the rival company to Shakespeare's Lord Chamberlain's Men, The Admiral's Men, for a decade or more.

Hoole described exactly how Mantuan, this Mantuan who so inspired Drayton and whom Holofernes so loved, was taught:

> For afternoon lessons on Mondays and Wednesdays, let them make use of Mantuanus, which is a poet both for style and matter, very familiar and grateful to children, and therefore read in most schools. They may read over some of the *Ecologues...* taking six lines at a lesson, which they should first commit to memory, as they are able. Secondly, Construe. Thirdly, Parse. Then help them to pick out the Phrases and Sentences (i.e. *sententiae*), which they may commit to a paper-book; and afterwards resolve the matter of their lessons into an English period or two, which they may turn into proper and elegant Latin, observing the placing of words, according to prose.

The boys memorized their six lines of Mantuan's poetry, then analyzed them by construing and parsing, then chose a phrase or sentence to write in their copy books, then translated the sentence into English prose, then turned it back into Latin prose. Reading, memorizing, analyzing, parsing, construing, translating into elegant Latin – again and again.

---

71.   Stopes, 208.

Baldwin noted that Mantuan was held in such high esteem, was looked at with such "awesome dignity," that Shakespeare would have shocked his audiences by making light of him as he did through the character of Holofernes. Indeed, Shakespeare probably enjoyed doing just that and has had the last laugh over the era's serious, overly erudite tutors, teachers, and university wits ever since.

Though not mentioned by Hoole, scholars have found allusions in Shakespeare to the *Colloquies* of Helvicus and the *Zodiacus Vitae* of Palingenius, another of the Renaissance moral poets studied in school. When the boys were ten or so, they were introduced through Palingenius to the image of the world's being a stage. The image was developed in the wildly popular *Zodiacus Vitae* (first in printed 1531*).* The metaphor became a commonplace of the time, though we of course tend to connect it solely with Shakespeare. He immortalized it in *As You Like It* (Jaques: "All the world's a stage and all the men and women merely players..."), but he had already rehearsed it in *The Merchant of Venice* when Antonio observes: "I hold the world but as the world, Gratiano/ A stage where every man must play a part/ And mine a sad one."

Less familiar is its use in Northumberland's comment from *Henry IV Part 2*:

> Let order die!
>
> And let this world no longer be a stage
>
> To feed contention in a lingering act.

Henry IV Part 2 Act I Scene 1

Its first appearance in Shakespeare's work is in Sonnet #15:

When I consider everything that grows

Holds in perfection but a little moment,

That this huge stage presenteth nought but shows

Whereon the stars in secret influence comment...

To divide the life of man into parts was another common device. Ovid and Horace in the Roman era and Palingenius in the Renaissance explored the life of man in six or seven stages. Ovid observed that man is born, he learns to crawl, he learns to stand and walk, he experiences youth, middle age, declines, and grows old. These divisions, which had been studied and discussed in Shakespeare's school, resurfaced decades later as the bitter Jacques reflected on human life in the otherwise idyllic forest of Arden (*As You Like It* Act II scene 7).

One of Palingenius's poems included the following:

But when once our life has faded into thin air, we are nothing, as if we had not been born... whatsoever things have arisen fall: what things have begun will see an end. Mighty cities and peoples, powerful realms, the highest mountains and the greatest rivers, time bears away, and shalt thou, vilest of dust, exist for ever? So great is the confidence of an ill-equipped mind. Forsooth, we labour in vain in the love of virtue, by hoping dreams and by inventing chimeras.

In *The Tempest*, the images of Palingenius came through Shakespeare's memory to help form the thoughts of Prospero:

Our revels now are ended. These our actors,

As I foretold you, were all spirits and

Are melted into air, into thin air:

And like the baseless fabric of this vision,

The cloud-capp'd towers, the gorgeous palaces,

The solemn temples, the great globe itself,

Yea, all which it inherit, shall dissolve

And like this insubstantial pageant faded,

Leave not a rack behind. We are such stuff

As dreams are made on, and our little life

Is rounded in a sleep.

The Tempest Act IV scene 1

If Shakespeare had left school at age ten, he would already have learned much to inform his later thinking. His imagination was filled with images; he had been given language patterns to express them. But there was more to come. He now left the usher behind, moved with his classmates to the front of the room, and, in the upper forms, started his work with Schoolmaster Jenkins.

CHAPTER 7

SCHOOLBOOKS IN THE UPPER FORMS

Lily's *Grammar*, the *New Testament*, and Ovid's *Metamorphoses,* were books Shakespeare was introduced to young and used to the end of his schooling. But, year by year, and form by form, new authors were introduced. While it must be stressed that we cannot claim with certitude exactly what books, authors, or teaching techniques were used at the King Edward VI School in Stratford, from observations of other schools, and from what is revealed in his plays and poems, we can assume that, in his Upper School experience, Shakespeare was taught from the standard list of texts. The books discussed below gave the boys material for their themes, variations, epistles, and orations—exercises we examined in Chapter 4.

FOURTH FORM

> Continue with Lily and the Testament; add Cicero's *Epistles,* Ovid's *Metamorphoses* and *De Tristibus,* Terence's *Elements of Rhetoric* and Buchanan's *Psalms.*

Hoole says that in "The fourth form... for after-noon lessons they read Terence two days, and Mantuan two days, which they translated into English, and repeated on Fridays, as before."

Terence and Mantuan were old companions. New to the boys were Cicero's *Epistles* and Buchanan's *Psalms.*

Reading Cicero's epistles acquainted the boys with many kinds of letters as well as giving them an elegant style of Latin to emulate. But the letters also made the history of Rome in the age of Julius Caesar come alive. Drawing upon Plutarch's *Lives of the Ancient Greeks and Romans*[72] for the conclusion of *Julius Caesar*, Shakespeare also had the relationship between Cicero and the conspirators, Brutus and Messalla, fixed in his imagination because of letters like this, the last letter of Cicero (#36), written to Brutus shortly before Brutus's suicide:

> "To M. Iunius Brutus (in Macedonia) Rome, Middle of July, 43 B.C.
>
> You have Messalla with you... beware of thinking, Brutus... that he has any parallel in honesty and firmness, care and zeal for the Republic.... Grieved as I was to let him go from my side, my one consolation was that in going to you, who are to me a second self, he was performing a duty and following the path of the truest glory. But enough of this...
>
> What is really pressing, Brutus, is that you should come to Italy with your army as soon as possible. There is the greatest anxiety for your arrival. Directly you reach Italy all classes will flock to you. For if we win the victory... there will be need of your counsel in establishing some form of constitution. And even if there is still some fighting left to be done, our greatest hope is both in your personal influence and in the material strength of your army. But make haste, in God's name! You know the importance of seizing the right moment, and of rapidity.
>
> What pains I am taking in the interests of your sister's children, I hope you know... In undertaking their cause I show more regard to your affection, which is very precious to me, than, as some think, to my own consistency. But there

---

72.   See Appendix C.

is nothing in which I more wish to be and to seem consistent than in loving you."[73]

How ironic that the letters of Cicero should have survived 1,500 years to inspire the Elizabethans, whereas none from Shakespeare, not yet 500 years in our past, exist to enlighten us. But Cicero was a public figure whose works were preserved as historical records. Shakespeare was a playwright, working at a job no one respected, the nature of which was ephemeral—a man whose work was not considered to be of literary or historic interest until years after his death.

George Buchanan, a Scot, was one of the finest Latin writers of the 16th century. He was a contemporary of Shakespeare's teachers, a man who had studied in Paris and translated tragedies into Latin from the Greek. He was tutor to Michel de Montaigne in France and, in Scotland, to both Mary Queen of Scots and her son (who would become James the First in England and Shakespeare's patron). Buchanan had written a history of Scotland and had translated two of the Greek tragedies, but he was known particularly for his Latin versifications of the *Psalms*.

The boys in school studied Buchanan's *Psalms* to measure his Latin against that of Terence. As Alice Fort and Herbert Kates note:

> Terence supplied the standard of classical Latin for many centuries. He was studied and acted even during those dark periods when all semblance of art seems to have died out in Europe... The prologues of Terentian plays contain valuable criticism and statements of dramatic principles.

73.   Cicero, *The Letters of Cicero*. http:www.fordham.edu/halsal1/ ancient/cicero-letters.asp

His sententious sayings have become the general property
of mankind: 'Many men, many minds!' 'I consider nothing
human alien to me,' and 'While there's life there's hope.' It is
through Terence, more than any one else, that the traditions
of comedy can be traced back to the New Comedy of the
Greeks."[74]

Terence's plays were admired and performed by young
scholars, but anyone who summarized wisdom in brief
sayings ripe for memorization, analyzing, and translating
seemed to have found a place in the Elizabethan
schoolroom.

FIFTH FORM

Ovid's *Metamorphoses,* Tully's (Cicero's) *Offices* and
Rheorica Ad Herennium; Florus's *Poetarum*;... Livy's
Orations, Caesar's *Commentaries*; Virgil's *Eclogues*
and *Odes*; Susenbrotus's *Schemes and Tropes*; Sallust;
Aphthonius's *Progymnasmatae.*

According to Hoole:

The fifth form said one part in the Latin, and another in the
Greek Grammar together;[75] their after-noons Lessons were
two days in Ovid's *Metamorphosis*, and two days Tully's
[Cicero's] *Offices*, both which they translated into English;
they learned to scan and prove verses in Florus *Poetarum*,
and repeated their week's works on Fridays, as before.

The enormous number of references to Ovid in
Shakespeare's works are traced in detail by H.E.D. Anders in
his thesis *Shakespeare's Books,*[76] and a detailed description

---

74.   *Minute History of the Drama,* 84-88.
75.   Though Hoole started Greek in the Fifth Form, other evidence shows many
       schools waited till the Sixth Form to begin Greek.
76.   http://archive.org/stream/bookshakespeare00andeuoft_djvu. txt

of Shakespeare's use of Ovid is found in Appendix D of this book. So we'll concentrate here on the *Rhetorica Ad Herennium*. In the first page, the boys were reminded how Cicero constructed a persuasive message:

> "The Introduction is the beginning of the discourse, and by it the hearer's mind is prepared for attention.
>
> Narration or Statement of Facts sets forth the events that have occurred or might have occurred.
>
> By means of the Division we make clear what matters are agreed upon and what are contested, and announce what points we intend to take up.
>
> Proof is the presentation of our arguments, together with their corroboration.
>
> Refutation is the destruction of all our adversaries' arguments.
>
> The Conclusion is the end of the discourse, formed in accordance with the principles of the art."[77]

A cursory look at Mark Antony's speech in the third act of *Julius Caesar* shows how well Shakespeare mastered his Cicero.

To Susenbrotus and his *Schemes and Tropes*, Livy's *Orations*, and the *Odes* and *Eclogues* of Virgil, the boys now added Sallust. A historian of the time of Caesar, Sallust was best known for his *Bellum Catilinae*, a monograph about the conspiracy of Catiline. He was admired by Tacitus and Quintilian (who in turn were admired by Elizabethan educators). Sallust, often compared to both Thucydides

---

77.   http://penelope.uchicago.edu/Thayer/E/Roman/Texts/Rhetorica_ad_
       Herennium/1*.html

and Livy, would have appealed to Shakespeare, as the historian was interested not just in chronicling events, but in the nature of a man's character, and the connection between character, action, and events.

Caesar was not neglected—particularly his *Commentaries*, which Shakespeare referred to at least twice, first in the following passage in *Henry VI Part 2*, Act IV:

> Kent, in the *Commentaries* Caesar writ,
>
> Is termed the civil'st place of all this isle:
>
> Sweet is the country, because full of riches;
>
> The people liberal, valiant, active, wealthy.

and then in *Richard III* (Act III):

> That Julius Caesar was a famous man;
>
> With what his valour did enrich his wit,
>
> His wit set down to make his valour live;
>
> Death makes no conquest of this conqueror;
>
> For now he lives in fame, though not in life.[78]

THE *PROGYMNASMATA*

For a detailed study of rhetorical devices, the schoolmaster turned the attention of his students to Aphthonius and his *Progymnasmata*.

Aphthonius made a list of 14 exercises preparatory to constructing orations *(gymnasmatae)*. They were listed

---

78.   Anders, Chapter 1.

in order of difficulty and the boys worked through them progressively. These *progymnasmatae* included the following structures:

Fable

Narrative

Chreia

Proverb

Refutation

Confirmation

Commonplace

Encomium

Vituperation

Comparison

Impersonation

Description

Thesis

Defend/Attack a Law[79]

Each of these came with a series of steps to guide the boys as they wrote them, and prepared to speak or perform them.

---

79.   http://rhetoric.byu.edu/pedagogy/progymnasmata/ Progymnasmata.htm

Take *chreia*, for instance. The term means "a brief reminiscence referring to some person in a pithy form for the purpose of edification." It takes the form of an anecdote that reports either a saying, an edifying action, or both. The boys would be told to amplify a brief account of what someone has said or done, using the following steps (the Latin name of each reminds us again that all this work was done in Latin):

1. Praise the sayer or doer, or what he has done
laudativus

2. Give a paraphrase of the theme
paraphrasticus

3. Say why this was said or done
causa

4. Introduce a contrast
contrarium

5. Introduce a comparison
parabola

6. Give an example of the meaning
exemplum

7. Support the saying/action with testimony of others
testimonium veterum

8. Conclude with a brief epilogue or conclusion
brevis epilogus[80]

Here is an example of *chreia* from *Julius Caesar*, written by Shakespeare about 1599.

---

80.   Baldwin, *Shakspere's Small Latine*, 1, 221.

CASSIUS

Well, honour is the subject of my story...

I was born free as Caesar; so were you:
laudativus

We both have fed as well, and we can both

Endure the winter's cold as well as he:
paraphrasticus

For once, upon a raw and gusty day,

The troubled Tiber chafing with her shores,

Caesar said to me 'Darest thou, Cassius, now
causa

Leap in with me into this angry flood,

And swim to yonder point?' Upon the word,

Accoutred as I was, I plunged in

And bade him follow; so indeed he did.

The torrent roar'd, and we did buffet it

With lusty sinews, throwing it aside

And stemming it with hearts of controversy;

But ere we could arrive the point proposed,

Caesar cried 'Help me, Cassius, or I sink!'
contrarium

I, as Aeneas, our great ancestor,

Did from the flames of Troy upon his shoulder

The old Anchises bear, so from the waves of Tiber
parabola

Did I the tired Caesar. And this man

Is now become a god, and Cassius is
exemplum

A wretched creature and must bend his body,

If Caesar carelessly but nod on him.

He had a fever when he was in Spain,
contrarium

And when the fit was on him, I did mark

How he did shake: 'tis true, this god did shake;

His coward lips did from their colour fly,
exemplum

And that same eye whose bend doth awe the world

Did lose his lustre: I did hear him groan:

Ay, and that tongue of his that bade the Romans
testimonium

Mark him and write his speeches in their books,

Alas, it cried 'Give me some drink, Titinius,'
contrarium, exemplum

As a sick girl. Ye gods, it doth amaze me

A man of such a feeble temper should
brevis epilogus

So get the start of the majestic world

And bear the palm alone.

Julius Caesar Act I Scene 2[81]

It is easy to see how working through all fourteen of these rhetorical structures repeatedly could take a great deal of time and would fix both intention and form in a student's mind. We are reminded that Shakespeare did not invent the oratorical structures in his plays. To formulate his ideas, he consciously and systematically applied techniques learned in school.

SIXTH FORM

> *The Greek Grammar* of Cleonard, *The Little Greek Catechism* set forth by public authority or any other good Author in Greek, *St. John's Gospel* plus *Virgil* and Cicero/Tully's *Orations,* Seneca's *Tragedies.*

Hoole takes us into the Sixth Form:

> The sixth form continued their parts in the Greek *Grammar,* and formed a verb Active at every part; they read the *Greek Testament* for fore-noons Lessons, beginning with *Saint John's Gospel*; their after-noons Greek began in the sixth form, using *The Greek Grammar* of Cleonard. Lessons were scheduled for two days in Virgil, and two days in Tully's *Orations.* They construed the Greek Testament into Latin, and the rest into English.

The longer the list of schoolbooks becomes, the more likely it seems that selections from authors were read, not

---

81.   See *Henry IV Part I* for Hotspur's tale of why he wants to keep his prisoners for another one (of many) examples.

complete works. But one author's eminence demanded the study of whole plays: Seneca and his *Tragedies*. Brian Arkins observes that Shakespeare derived from Seneca the following seven general features:

1. An obsession with *scelus*, crime.

2. A preoccupation with torture, mutilation, incest and corpses—as in *Titus Andronicus.*

3. A stress on witchcraft and the supernatural—as in *Macbeth.*

4. The existence of vaulting ambition in the prince—as in *Richard III* and *Macbeth.*

5. The ghost that calls for revenge—as in *Hamlet* and *Macbeth.*

6. The self-dramatization of the hero, especially as he dies—as in *Hamlet* and *Macbeth.*

7.The frequent use of stichomythia in dialogue—as in *Richard III* and *Hamlet.*[82]

Arkins continues: "The revenge play, which is launched by *scelus*, comes in three phases, consisting of: 1. the appearance of the ghost or Fury; 2. the making of the revenger; and 3. the ritual revenge itself..." [83]

We see this pattern in the plays noted by Arkins as "Shakespeare's most Senecan": *Titus Andronicus, Hamlet, Richard III,* and *Macbeth.*

---

82.   Arkins, section 3.
83.   Ibid., section 4. The plays of Seneca most contributing to these according to Arkins are *The Trojan Women, Phaedra, Thyestes, Agamemnon* and *Hercules Furens.*

In addition to Seneca, the tragedian, we must note the great writer of Roman comedy, Plautus, whose *Manaechmi* Shakespeare used so directly in *The Comedy of Errors*. Plautus, Terence, and Seneca are authors Shakespeare first met in school, and they are among those he continued reading into adulthood.[84]

OTHER BOOKS AND LITERARY WORKS REFLECTED IN SHAKESPEARE'S WRITING

Before reaching the Seventh or Eighth Form (if indeed these were even included at the Stratford school), Shakespeare would—probably to his relief—have found his schooldays over.

But Shakespeare never stopped reading. For his English history plays (a third of his output) we see him draw from English dramatic works and literature—especially from Raphael Holinshed's *The Chronicles of England, Scotlande, and Ireland* (1577) and Edward Hall's *The vnion of the two noble and illustre famelies of Lancastre & Yorke*. Similarly, for his tragedies set in the ancient world, he used Plutarch's *Lives of the Ancient Greeks and Romans*, and Ovid's *Metamorphoses*.

He saw and/or read the plays of Marlowe, Lyly, Kyd, Peele, Nashe, Greene, and his other contemporaries in London. He remembered the Mystery and Morality plays produced in his childhood at Coventry.

---

84.   Other authors read in Tudor schools included the Romans Justinus (Justin), Suetonius (*The Lives of the Twelve Caesars*), Livy (*Orations*), Q. Curtius (*Alexander the Great*), Sedulius, Juvenal Heliodorus, Marianus, Quintilian, and Pliny. The Jewish historian Josephus was well-known, as was Homer; and, among the moderns, Erasmus was widely read (*Copia* and *Colloquies*).

It was an age when more and more people were learning to read, and the Elizabethan book trade thrived. Romantic stories were very popular; Shakespeare had access to those of Arthur, Guy, Bevis, and Lodge.

Ballads had a huge audience: long poems telling romantic stories that were sold in sheets—tales of Robin Hood, Cophetua, Susanna, Jephthah, and more. Songs, including roundelays and jigs, were printed and sold (note Autolychus in *The Winter's Tale* singing and marketing his song sheets). Popular tales, proverbs, and folklore were everywhere available.

When Shakespeare came to write *Venus and Adonis* and *The Rape of Lucrece,* he first turned for inspiration to Ovid, but then had the serious poems of Christopher Marlowe, Samuel Daniel, Edmund Spencer, and Philip Sidney—to say nothing of Chaucer[85]—to compare to his own. In addition, there were prose writings of Lyly, Sidney, Harsnet, Raleigh, Eden, and more.

French authors were translated into English and were well disseminated: Montaigne, in Florio's translation, was a favorite of Shakespeare's, but there were also Ronsard and Rabelais.

Commenting on Shakespeare's reading, A. L. Rowse observes that, though Shakespeare drew from Ovid and the *Bible,* it was the first book of the *Metamorphoses* that he knew the best, and the earliest chapters of the *Old* and *New Testaments* with which he was most deeply

---

85.   Rowse, *My View of Shakespeare,* 38. Rowse says, "From the sonnets we know that William was reading Chaucer, in a new edition recently out, and, from *The Knight's Tale* was minded to write a 'midsummer story.'"

acquainted. "His mind," observed Rowse, "was not that of a scholar, pursuing these things as an end in themselves... but that of a poet."

> Very often it was the words themselves that got fixed in his mind, to come out again by a process of unconscious association. The phrase in Ovid, *rudis indigestaque moles*, fastened on his ear to pop out again at different times in his writing: Richard III is described as a
>
> Heap of wrath, *foul undigested lump*.
>
> After the chaos of King John's reign, his son is hailed as born
>
> To set a form upon that *indigest*
>
> Which he hath left *so shapeless and so rude*.

And Rowse continues:

> The plain fact is that Shakespeare had a fabulous aural memory -- nothing like it in the whole of literature: he heard a phrase at school, like Quintilian's *universis... largitur;* it comes out years later as *'largess universal'*. It is not a common cliché but an association; it was the word, the phrase, that's transfixed him. This is the first, though by no means the last, sign of the poet; but no one has ever had it as he had.[86]

Shakespeare's petty school teachers and grammar school masters taught him to read English, then to read and write Latin; they gave him access to literature rich in images to fill his mind, and skills to structure action and vary language. He continued the habit of reading his entire life, basing his plays on stories he read, always looking for sources that would inspire and feed his extraordinary imagination. The

---

86.   Ibid.

masters at the King Edward IV School would surely agree that whether or not William Shakespeare enjoyed school, the young scholar had learned his lessons well.

CHAPTER 8

HANDWRITING, MUSIC, ARITHMETIC

"...and some hours they shall learn to sing and to write." [87]

Handwriting, music, and arithmetic were skills that Shakespeare acquired in his youth, but teaching them had no place in most of the daily schedules that have come down to us. Children learned handwriting in petty school, but it is difficult to believe the practice stopped there. Music was a universal experience, but we don't know that much about how and where it was taught. The "casting of accounts," a rudimentary form of bookkeeping, was confined to petty school and seems to represent the sum of the attention given arithmetic, but higher mathematics was studied intently at the university level. Somehow, children learned more than the rudiments of these subjects. So, though they were not alluded to in the fundamental grammar school curriculum, we will take a brief look at these areas; they were, after all, a part of Shakespeare's education and references to them showed up in his plays.

HANDWRITING

In their dedication to the *First Folio*, Shakespeare's friends John Heminges and Henry Condell wrote, "His mind and his hand went together; and what he thought, he uttered with that easiness, that we have scarce received from him a blot in his papers." To not blot one's papers was a considerable accomplishment. To have no blots meant to

---

87.   Baldwin, *Shakspere's Small Latine,* 1: 351.

have well trimmed pen nibs cut with a sharp pen knife, to change pens often, to use high-quality ink, to dip the pen and write with care, and to dry the ink (using fine sand, called "dust," or blotting papers) with equal concern. It would appear Shakespeare cared about the physical act of writing.

Children had to develop this skill by the age of seven in order to start grammar school. In *The Petie Schole,* Francis Clement said of the children coming to him: "The writer must provide ... paper, ink, pen, penknife, ruler, desk, and dust box, of these the three first are most necessary, the four latter very requisite."

William Kempe, in his *The Education of Children,* describes the process.

> The master shall teach his scholar to write by precepts of holding the pen, of forming the letters in due proportion, of joining them aptly together: by practice of drawing the pen upon the figures of shadowed letters, then of writing without shadowed letters by imitating a copie, lastly, of writing without a copie. In this exercise of writing, the scholar shall spend but two or three hours in a day at the most, employing the rest of the time in reading, until he be about seven years old.[88]

But according to the information published by the Shakespeare Birthplace Trust,

> ... it is clear from schoolmasters' complaints that many did not have the basic skills and had to acquire them at grammar school. In large towns boys were sent at the end of the morning and afternoon to a writing master who set copies and criticized previous efforts, while in country

---

88.   Baldwin, *Shakspere's Petty School,* 11-12 (modernized spelling mine).

grammar schools the pupils were usually taught intensively by a travelling scrivener who would spend a month or six weeks each year at the school.[89]

So the physical practice of writing was apparently worked into and around the daily school schedule.[90]

The boys could make their own ink,[91] or buy it from an apothecary or stationer. It was transported and held at one's desk in an inkhorn. Though this probably meant an actual vessel made of horn in early days, by Shakespeare's time it referred to an ink container of wood, ivory, or glass—with a stopper, or lid, that fit tightly so that the ink would not spill.[92]

The boys would also bring quill pens to school or to the writing master.[93] These could come from swans, turkeys, pheasants, ravens, pelicans, even peacocks. But the best type of quill for a playwright who cared about how his

89. Shakespeare Birthplace Trust, "Writing in Elizabethan Schools," 2011: 1.

90. Brinsley's *Ludus Literarius: or, the Grammar Schoole* contains a detailed chapter on teaching children to write.

91. Ibid., Two versified recipes for ink making:
To make comon yncke, of wyne take a quarte.
To ounces of gumme, let that be apart,
Five ounces of Galles, of copros take three,
Long standing doth make it better to bee:
If wyne ye do want, rayne water is best,
And then as much stuffe as above at the least:
If ynke be too thicke, put vinegre in:
For water doth make the colour more dimme.
To make yncke in haste
In haste, for a shift when ye have great neede.
Take woll, or wollen to stand you in steade.
Which burnt in the fire, the powder beate small
With vinegre, or water make yncke withall.

92. http://www.threadsofhistory.com/Eowyn/EowynsEncheiridion/ScribalTools. htlml. This site has many drawings of inkhorns and penners illustrating well how they looked and functioned.

93. In *Love's Labour's Lost*, Don Armodo says: "I did encounter that obscene and preposterous event, that draweth from my snow-white pen the ebon-coloured ink."

writing looked came from the third or fourth feathers on the wing of a goose. (Quills from the left wing of the goose lay most easily in the hand of a right-handed writer and therefore claimed a higher price).[94]

On his way to school, a boy carried his pens and penknife in a container called a penner: a rectangular holder made of wood or leather. The inkhorn was attached to the penner by cords that allowed the implements to be hung from the belt, penner on one side, inkhorn on the other.

At each boy's desk was a hole into which the inkhorn or bottle would fit for easy dipping, while the quill pens stood in holders called "quill holes..."[95] On the writer's desk, there would also be paper, sold by the quire (twenty-four or twenty-five sheets), the aforementioned fine sand ("dust") in a box or shaker, and perhaps blotting paper.[96]

Elizabethans didn't always sit at a desk to write. They also took notes on the run. A generation before Shakespeare, Vives suggested: "Make a book of blank leaves of a proper size. Divide it into certain topics... names of subjects of daily converse... rare words, idioms, maxims, difficult passages in authors, matters of note. So that thou shalt have all these noted down and digested."[97] Shakespeare referred to this habit in *Hamlet,* when the prince pulled out his notebook ("tables") and said: "Meet it is I write it down. That one may smile and smile and be a villain."[98]

---

94.   Nickel, 3-5.
95.   Nickel, 16. There were also quill-cleaners: containers made of silver or porcelain containing lead shot or bristles which would clean the inserted quill tip.
96.   First mentioned in 1465.
97.   Baldwin, *Shakspere's Small Latine* 1:189.
98.   In the collection of the Morgan Library in New York, there is a small white notebook approximately the size of a deck of cards. With it is a silverpoint stylus, and the information says that the paper of the notebook is treated so

But knowing how to write in Medieval or even Early Modern England was not universally admired. Shakespeare was well aware of this attitude when he wrote *Henry VI Part 2:*

CADE
Is not this a lamentable thing, that of the skin of an innocent lamb should be made parchment? that parchment, being scribbled o'er, should undo a man?...

How now! who's there?

Enter some, bringing forward the Clerk of Chatham

SMITH
The clerk of Chatham: he can write and read and cast accompt.

CADE
O monstrous!

SMITH
We took him setting of boys' copies.[99]

CADE
Here's a villain!... Dost thou use to write thy name? or hast thou a mark to thyself, like an honest plain-dealing man?

CLERK
Sir, I thank God, I have been so well brought up that I can write my name.

ALL
He hath confessed: away with him! he's a villain and a traitor.

---

that notes can be taken with the stylus, kept as long as needed, then rubbed out gently. The surface, it is claimed, becomes clear again within fifteen minutes.

99.   It seems the Clerk was also a teacher who gave the boys writing assignments.

CADE
Away with him, I say! hang him with his pen and inkhorn
about his neck.

Exit one with the Clerk

For the Clerk, this was indeed his final exit.

On the other hand, proof of being able to read once saved
the life of Shakespeare's colleague Ben Jonson. Jonson
was imprisoned for murder after killing a fellow actor in a
duel; he claimed "benefit of clergy." Under this provision, a
man would be spared capital punishment if he could prove
literacy by reading from the *Bible*. Jonson had no trouble
demonstrating his reading skills, and so education fatal to
the clerk in Shakespeare's play was salvation to his friend
the playwright.

MUSIC

Music with tunes, delights the ear
And makes us think it heaven
Arithmetic by number can make
Reckonings to be even.
Wilson's *Rule of Reason*, 1562[100]

John Sturm, writing of an annual school examination in
1578, said that in the Sixth Form, "we have attended to
the science of time" in the first book of music..."[101] James
Whitelocke remarked on Richard Mulcaster's teaching of
music "I was brought up at School under Mr. Mulcaster...
. His care was also to increase my skill in music, in which

---

100.   Quoted in Plimpton, 121.
101.   Ibid., 293.

I was brought up by daily exercise in it, as in singing and playing upon instruments..." Brinsley suggested singing as a break in the school day, for recreation;[102] one stipulation for the Parker scholarship that enabled Christopher Marlowe to go to Cambridge was that the scholars be "so entred into the skill of song that they shall at first sight solf and sing plaine song."[103]

Apparently, then, music was very much a part of the school experience even though the schedules we've found so far do not specifically mention it. From the requirement that boys bring with them to school a book of the metrical psalms, as mentioned in previous chapters, we can assume that the boys were taught basic part-singing—and that they would sing again in church every Sunday.

We can imagine Shakespeare responding enthusiastically to musical instruction. Though he did not write tunes, he included songs in virtually every play; and all of them— even the tragedies—ended with a dance or jig (what we would think of as the curtain call). So popular were these dances that some members of the audience would skip the play altogether and come to see only the musical entertainment at the end.

There is no indication that the Stratford Grammar School specialized in musical training—not like the great cathedral schools, whose choirs were schooled intensively in the art. In a local grammar school, music might be emphasized or given short shrift, depending on the background and interest of the schoolmaster.

---

102.   Brinsley, 299.
103.   *Oxford Dictionary of National Biography,* Marlowe.

Nonetheless, musical skill was an expected accomplishment. In *The Compleat Gentleman* (1634), Henry Peacham says: " I desire no more in you than to sing your part sure, and at the first sight, withal, to play the same upon your Viol or the exercise of the Lute, privately to your self." [104]

If music was not offered in the local school, music masters gave private instruction to those who could afford it. Instructors were not hard to find. When the monasteries were closed in the mid-16th century, many musicians lost their employment and were readily available for private tutorial work.[105] In *The Taming of the Shrew* Shakespeare gave an idea of how music was taught (i.e., by use of the "gamut") in the mock lesson Hortensio, the fake music master, offered as he wooed Bianca.

HORTENSIO

Madam, before you touch the instrument,

To learn the order of my fingering,

I must begin with rudiments of art;

To teach you gamut...

And there it is in writing, fairly drawn.

BIANCA

Why, I am past my gamut long ago.

---

104.   Peacham, 100.
105.   Long, 26.

HORTENSIO

Yet read the gamut of Hortensio.

BIANCA

[Reads] "Gamut' I am, the ground of all accord,

'A re,' to Plead Hortensio's passion;

'B mi,' Bianca, take him for thy lord,

'C fa ut,' that loves with all affection:

'D sol re,' one clef, two notes have I:

'E la mi,' show pity, or I die.'

Call you this gamut? tut, I like it not:

Old fashions please me best; I am not so nice,

To change true rules for old inventions.

(Taming of the Shrew Act III Scene 1)

The "gamut" was a basic solfegio technique, enabling the singer to read music at sight and sing correct intervals. Shakespeare would have learned its rudiments as the boys sang their daily psalms.

ARITHMETIC

"Writing and the casting of accounts, with pen and counters, was to be taught holidays and Saturdays."[106]

---

106.   Stowe, 135.

This quote from the statutes in the town of Bungay indicates that basic arithmetic was addressed, though not during regular school hours.

In fact, the skill of casting accounts could be acquired by people who missed out on petty school or grammar school—even, therefore, by those who were not literate. The author of a classic French book of accounting (*The Liure des Getez,* c. 1510) affirmed that "there are many merchants who can neither read nor write but who yet must be good at figure work."[107] A popular book of the time entitled *Arithmetica* said, "The practice of calculation by means of jettons [markers] is very useful to all money-changers, retail dealers, innkeepers, and numerous others of low estate, besides all such as through their own negligence or mental incapacity are unable to read, as is the case with many people of all conditions.[108]

This would describe John Shakespeare, William's father, who was a successful businessman and was twice elected Chamberlain of the Stratford Corporation (i.e., town Treasurer), although he used only a mark to sign his name. When William Shakespeare worked in his father's glove shop, he would have seen his father casting accounts and in this way he would have learned from simple observation arithmetic skills not taught in school. The practice involved the use of casters—also called markers, counters, or jettons—and a flat surface onto which were drawn lines to form a grid. Tossing the counters into the correct squares of the grid became a skill necessary to balance his books.[109]

---

107.   Hain, footnote, 154.
108.   Ibid., quoting Siliceus.
109.   In *The Medieval Account Books of the Mercers of London,* Lisa Jefferson describes the ritualized yearly procedure for this trade guild that persisted until the eighteenth century:

A woodcut appears in the 1543 edition showing four men around a square table, one seated and pointing to a grid on which are placed counters.

The dominant arithmetic book of the day was by the mathematician Robert Recorde. Published in the early 1540s, *Arithmetick, or The Ground of Artes: teaching the worke and practise of arithmetike, moch necessary for all states of men,* was the first book of arithmetic ever printed in English.

Recorde was equally known for a second book called *The Whetstone of Witte,* published in 1557. This book is noted for introducing the equal sign into mathematics, "And to avoid the tedious repetition of these words 'is equal to,' I will set as I do often in work use a pair of parallels or... lines of one length, thus =, because no two things can be more equal."

Recorde wrote a little verse to introduce the idea behind this book:

Here, if you list your wittes to whette,

Moche sharpenesse thereby shall you gette.[110]

The calculations, later recorded in writing, were done on an abacus or a chequer board (as at the Exchequer). During the accounting and audit ceremony, the various monies received by the wardens would be set out as counters upon one part of the board, and then afterwards counters representing the amounts they had paid out for various items would be placed on another part of the board. Sum totals for each were reckoned, one figure taken from the other and a balance arrived at. This balance then had to be handed over to the new wardens. Details of all receipts and expenditures, and of debts, were provided on paper sheets in a quire, or in a loosely bound record book and mention is quite often made that these details have been exhibited for confirmation and authorization.

110. Re *The Whetstone of Witte*:
      Many are now puzzled by the title of this book, which is in fact a rather nifty pun, only funny when either it is explained or one is well versed in Latin. *Cosa* is the

Shakespeare's knowledge of Recorde is revealed in *As You Like It* Act I Scene 1 when Celia says

> ... for always the dullness of the fool is the
>
> whetstone of the wits.

Celia and her cousin Rosalind are two of Shakespeare's best-educated and wittiest women—trained in arithmetic as well as language, it would seem.[111]

This varied system of learning these skills is full of curious twists and turns.

One, since the petty school was open to both girls and boys, young girls were on an equal footing with their brothers, male cousins, and friends, and had the opportunity to learn basic computation. This would have enabled them to keep household accounts and the accounts of their family businesses.

For boys at grammar school, arithmetic was not part of the curriculum even though there was a growing interest in mathematics and science. A prominent mathematician of the age (and advisor to Queen Elizabeth), John Dee, was committed to exploring the connection between mathematics and astrology. To him, the abstraction of mathematical thinking had natural connections to a spiritual dimension. Coming from a similar mindset, medical doctors like Shakespeare's son-in-law John Hall, and like the famous London physician Simon Forman, were

---

Latin for "thing," which was used for the unknown in early algebra. Algebraists were therefore often termed cossists and algebra was known as the cossic art. *Cos* is the Latin for "whetstone". Thus, this book could be used to sharpen one's mathematical wit."   http:h2g2.com/dna/h2g2/ A7269690.

111.   http://threesixty360.wordpress.com/tag/robert-recorde

expected to cast horoscopes as part of a medical treatment program.[112] In Shakespeare's life, the theatre itself was a metaphor for this instinct. The need of the poet and the actor "to give to airy nothing a local habitation and a name" speaks to a longing of the time to unite the physical and the spiritual.

But for the most part, references to arithmetic in Shakespeare's work don't go beyond the rudimentary abilities taught in petty school: in *The Comedy of Errors,* the buying and selling of the gold chain, the passing around of the purse of money, the entrusting of money to Dromio to buy the rope, all reflected the simple, day-to-day business transactions Shakespeare and his family observed and took part in in Stratford and London. Shakespeare acknowledged other arithmetical realities such as the taking out of large-scale loans and the computation of interest in *The Merchant of Venice,* but he dealt with them in a cursory way not one suggesting a deep knowledge of mathematics.

Today, a stage director working on *The Taming of the Shrew* will come to the scene where Baptista needs to find out which of the men wooing his younger daughter would be the better marital investment. As each suitor bids for Bianca, the scene calls out for a physicalization of the bidding process. If the production is set in modern times, a hand-held phone or computer device might be utilized; if set in earlier days, a primitive calculator, or a period adding machine could be a useful prop. But setting the production in Shakespeare's own time would give the director an opportunity to stage a true "casting of accounts"—with a

---

112.   The casting of a horoscope was the first step in a treatment from Simon Forman. But John Hall did not deal in para-phenomena.

grid on a table top, or one scratched into the ground, and an eager Baptista tossing onto it markers to keep track of the transaction.

We might take a moment now to consider the other side of Shakespeare's character: not Shakespeare the writer, but Shakespeare the businessman. He was a shareholder of a theatre company, the Lord Chamberlain's Men, along with a group of other keen and successful businessmen. He understood money: bookkeeping and audits, income versus outgo, what made good investment choices—land, tithes, houses, and so forth. All this indicates a savvy financial mind that allowed him to prosper in what was then, as now, a very risky business.

His early education in the casting of accounts and his subsequent shareholding experience gave him an understanding of numbers that served him well in his professional life. At the age of thirty-three, William Shakespeare was able to buy one of the finest houses in Stratford, and eventually to retire there to a life of ease.

CHAPTER 9

FROM STRATFORD TO LONDON: SHAKESPEARE'S CONTINUING EDUCATION

My gentle Shakespeare,... he
Who casts to write a living line, must sweat,
(Such as thine are) and strike the second heat
Upon the Muses' anvil; turn the same,
(And himself with it) that he thinks to frame;
Or for the laurel, he may gain a scorn,
For a great Poet's made, as well as born –
And such wert thou.

Ben Jonson
Preface to the *First Folio* of Shakespeare's plays

William Shakespeare would have left the King Edward VI School in the late 1570s when he was somewhere between the ages of thirteen and fifteen. His family was suffering from a reversal of fortune that struck them when John Shakespeare's speculative wool dealings coincided with a collapse of the wool trade. As a young man starting out to seek his fortune in the world, he had no trade, no skill, no focus.

There are many suggestions as to what Shakespeare did from the time he left school until the time he settled in London about a decade later. Edgar Fripp insisted he worked in the law office of the Stratford town clerk.[113] Duff

---

113.   Fripp, *Shakespeare's Stratford*, 14.

Cooper wrote a book, *Sergeant Shakespeare*, proposing that he spent time in the army. John Aubrey said he was a schoolmaster in the country. Anne-Marie Edwards, in *Walking with William Shakespeare,* suggested the town where he taught was Dursley "in the shadow of Stichcombe Hill" beside the river Ewelme.[114]

Those who believe Shakespeare was a hidden Catholic offer the idea that, with the help of the schoolmaster who followed Thomas Jenkins (a man named John Cottom and a Catholic recusant), he went north to Lancashire to live with the Hoghton family, to be one of their players (called William Shakshafte) and to be a tutor for their children.

He might have spent some time working with his Uncle Henry, who farmed land just up the road from Stratford in Ingon and Snitterfield. He may simply have worked in his father's glove shop.[115]

He could have done any or all of these things, seeking here and there a place to belong and, as many adolescents have experienced in every age, to find himself.

His most serious misstep was to look for solace in romance. When he was eighteen, he learned he had made Anne Hathaway, the daughter of a family friend, pregnant. The

---

114.   Edwards, 69.
115.   Honan, 29. As Park Honan points out, Shakespeare knew a great deal about leather and leather working:
"In *The Merry Wives*, Slender swears 'by these gloves,' and Mistress Quickly enquires of him, 'Does he not wear a great round beard, like a glover's paring-knife?'. Romeo exclaims to his lady aloft, 'O, that I were a glove upon that hand,' and Romeo's rash, wittiest friend understands the pliable, soft quality of kid-skin—or cheveril —used for the best, costliest gloves: 'O, here's a wit of cheveril, that stretches from an inch narrow to an ell broad,' says Mercutio. 'Hang nothing but a calf's skin,' mocks the Bastard in King John, and allusions to sheep-skin, lamb-skin, fox-skin, dog-skin, and deer-skin in the plays might conjure up a whittawer's drying shed."

mores of the time made it imperative that they marry, and so William complicated his life by bringing a wife (eight years older than he, and expecting) into the home of a family already crowded with five children, one just two years older than the coming infant. Two years later, Anne bore twins; so at age twenty-one, Shakespeare was living at home with his parents, his three brothers and one sister, his wife and three children, with no steady, tolerable work and worse—no prospects.

In the year 1587, when Shakespeare turned twenty-three, five acting companies came though Stratford and gave performances. Two of them in particular were familiar to the town and to Shakespeare's family. The first company was Leicester's Men, whose sponsor was the Earl of Leicester, long-time confidant of Elizabeth I. A number of the Leicester's men had been touring on the Continent at this time, so the company was stretched thin. They had in their midst James Burbage, with whom Shakespeare's father had become acquainted years earlier when, as Bailiff of Stratford, he had first allowed the company to play in the town's Guild Hall. The second, the even more prestigious Queen's Men, were short an actor because one of their company had recently been killed in a duel. They, too, boasted actors in their company familiar to the Shakespeares from former tours.[116]

Since Shakespeare turned up in London a year or so later, 1587 may have marked the turning point in his life. The theatrical companies passing through Stratford demonstrated that men could and did earn a living putting

---

116.   Wilson, 67-69.

on plays. They also claimed prestige because they were attached to aristocratic households.

We have looked at how Shakespeare's grammar school education trained him in skills useful in playwriting: to write with equal facility in prose and verse; to employ figures of speech to diversify language and heighten its expressiveness; to develop great speeches using classical rhetorical structures; to shape dramatic action in the multi-scene, five-act play form; to search literary and historical sources for subject matter. We have also seen that during his years at school, Shakespeare gained experience in doing oral presentations, in both English and Latin, and in performing scenes from classical plays.

But no school could teach the professional and technical demands of the stage: how to work with a given group of actors; how to write for—and be inspired by—an individual performer; how to revise a text, depending on where the play was to be produced (indoors or outdoors? at the royal Court for Christmas revelries? on tour in the guild halls of small country towns? with a full complement of players or a cut-down touring company?) A playwright also learned how to take into account the expenses related to costumes and properties; how to double actors, using a single actor for a number of roles; how to adapt to changing styles and tastes of audiences; how to collaborate with other—often temperamental—writers; and how to write in ways that satisfied the whims of management.

These were the demands of the craft and, though they had not been taught him in school, Shakespeare adjusted to them quickly. He proved from his earliest works (*Henry VI*

Parts 1,2 and 3; Titus Andronicus; The Comedy of Errors; The Taming of the Shrew; Richard III) to have an unerring instinct for sources filled with dramatic action and ripe for creative development. The *Henry VI* plays, for example, were among his first efforts. They are thought by many scholars to be collaborations or the reworkings of existing plays. Using their effective if simplistic organization, Shakespeare could avoid the problems of creating dramatic structure (of which he later became a master) to concentrate on creating characters like Talbot, Jack Cade, Joan la Pucelle, Margaret of Anjou, and Henry the king, and to add over-arching and unifying themes to the simplistic, sequential dramatic structure typical of the time.[117]

The late 1580s and early 1590s were an unsettled theatrical time in London, a time when a number of talented actors moved from company to company, as needed and as cast, and when the plague descended to interrupt the actors' best laid plans. It was 1594 before the best of the available actors settled into two companies, the Admiral's Men, led by Philip Henslowe and Edward Alleyn; and the Lord Chamberlain's Men (later the King's Men), led by the Burbage family (father James and sons Richard and Cuthbert). This company had four other co-shareholders, all actors in the company. One of them was William Shakespeare.

When he joined the Lord Chamberlain's Men, Shakespeare functioned in the company as both performer and playwright. His acting skills were honed along with his playwriting skills in the years between 1588 and 1594, and so he began to write his plays out of his experience

---

117.   Lawrence V. Ryan's introduction to the Signet *Henry VI, 1,2,3,* 1967 and 1989, contains a rich discussion of this point.

as an actor. From year to year, he learned how to increase the power of a play's construction, and of its language, by acting out his own words, characters, and situations— and those of other writers. The importance of this practical education, that of an actor turned playwright, cannot be overstated by anyone trying to understand his craftsmanship and artistry.

SHAKESPEARE THE COLLABORATOR

The performances of *Henry VI,* paid for by Philip Henslowe throughout the year 1592, provide our first indication of Shakespeare's playwriting success. Henslowe kept a ledger (called a diary) where payments for *Henry VI* are consistently logged.

The diary is evidence that many plays of the time were written by multiple authors. The appetite for new plays was voracious, and managers were in constant need of fresh works. If one writer couldn't write fast enough, a team would be hired to share the job.[118]

The three playwrights referred to earlier —Thomas Kyd, Christopher Marlowe, and Ben Jonson—were not in Shakespeare's league as actors. And though they shared a common experience of grammar school education each took a different path to success as a professional

---

118.   This pattern repeated in the writing of opera in the 18th and 19th century, in writing for the early film industry in Hollywood during the first half of the 20th century, and exists now in the groups of writers teamed up to write the scripts for cable-generated television shows in America. In fact the commentaries that come with purchased series such as *The Sopranos, Deadwood, Friday Night Lights* and the like often include writers from the team talking about sitting around the writers' table dividing up their work— a clear parallel with the situation in Shakespeare's London. The group writing of dramatic works comes about whenever there is a performance industry hungry if not desperate for a huge supply of texts.

playwright. But all four took advantage of a change in dramatic structure inspired by two actors: Edward Alleyn and Richard Burbage.

Though little is known of Thomas Kyd, his *Spanish Tragedy* focused on the leading character, Heironimo. Kyd also wrote other plays, now lost, and died young, having been imprisoned and tortured for "lewd and mutinous libles."

His roommate in London, Marlowe (perhaps the real author of the libelous material), narrowly escaped similar imprisonment and torture. Though Marlowe also died young, he was prolific and much admired at the time. Marlowe created great starring roles for Edward Alleyn early on in the two parts of *Tamburlaine the Great*, and later in subsequent plays.

The works of both men provided Shakespeare with dramatic models. Kyd's work emphasized Senecan revenge and included all the sensational devices so appealing to Elizabethan audiences and so effective in the theatre. Shakespeare later developed many of these devices, particularly supernatural beings, dumbshows, and discovery scenes.

Jonathan Bate points out, in his introduction to *Richard III*, that Shakespeare arrived on the scene just as the young Richard Burbage was achieving fame as a star actor. Burbage's portrayals inspired Shakespeare to follow Kyd and Marlowe in focusing the structure of his plays on a leading character. This was a significant change from plays featuring the acting ensemble *(Henry VI Parts 1, 2, and 3, The Comedy of Errors)*. The focus on a central character made complicated plots easier to follow, and gave audiences the thrill of watching a major role, performed by a great actor, control the dynamics of the presentation.

Scholars currently emphasize Shakespeare's participation in dramatic collaborations. Less in this way is conjectured concerning Marlowe. Marlowe wrote his earliest works while still at Cambridge, and came to London with plays finished and ready for professional performance. He thus established himself from the start as an independent playwright with no need of a collaborator. He was also employed by Queen Elizabeth I's secret service, a distraction and perhaps a reason to keep his distance from his playwriting colleagues.

In contrast, Ben Jonson, though a volatile character like Marlowe, was an active and proven collaborator. Henslowe noted that in 1598, Jonson wrote *Hot Anger Soon Cold* with Henry Chettle; followed the next year by *Page of Plymouth* with Thomas Dekker, and *Robert II, the King of Scots Tragedy*, with Chettle, Dekker, and others. In 1604, he collaborated with John Marston and George Chapman on *Eastward, Ho!*[119] But other works—including *Volpone*, his greatest—seem to have sprung from his pen alone. In this, he is like Shakespeare.

Shakespeare did collaborate: *Two Noble Kinsmen* is credited to John Fletcher and William Shakespeare; *Pericles* to George Wilkins and William Shakespeare; *Henry VIII*, again co-written with John Fletcher; and *Timon of Athens*, a collaboration with Thomas Middleton. Two witches' songs and Hecate's speeches in *Macbeth* have been suggested

---

119.   *Oxford Dictionary of National Biography*, Jonson.

as interpolations from Middleton,[120] and Shakespeare's earliest works, the *Henry VI* plays, as we have noted, are in all likelihood re-workings of existing texts. A speech in *Sir Thomas More* is thought to be in Shakespeare's hand (and if so, it is the only extensive sample we have of his handwriting). The question of which parts of these works—and others—are by Shakespeare and which parts by someone else offers a gold mine for researchers. Analysts now have computers programmed to count and compare words and phrases between Shakespeare's plays and those of others, in an effort to see how they match up, and to divide the authorship of scenes, speeches, and lines systematically.

One thing is obvious. The collaborative works are among the weakest of the plays attributed to William Shakespeare. As such, they are less often performed and more difficult to make pleasing to an audience. His partnerships, however they functioned, did not lift another writer's work to his level. The greatest of his plays remain his alone in imagination, conception, and execution.

SHAKESPEARE THE REVISER

The greatest plays are also his in revision. The differences noted in Shakespeare's plays between quarto versions (early paperback publications) and the *First Folio* versions (the official publication of the plays after his death) reflect the mutability of dramatic writing. The script of a play is open for interpretation. Every time it is performed, it changes. When one version is captured and printed, the published script takes on the set-in-stone nature of a fixed

---

120.   Brian Vickers demolishes the idea that Middleton had a major hand in *Macbeth* in his article in the *Times Literary Supplement*, May 28, 2010.

text. But the minute a company starts to perform that text, changes will inevitably occur.

Take *King Lear* as an example. Shakespeare wrote an early version of the play, which was published in quarto form in 1608. By the time his friends John Heminges and Henry Condell published the *First Folio* in 1623, *King Lear* showed up without the scene on the heath where Lear constructs a mad trial of his evil daughters. From that day to this, critics, producers, directors, actors, and teachers have had to struggle with the question, "Which is the 'real' *Lear*?" And more particularly, should the play be produced with or without the scene in question?

Shakespeare and his company are no help here. It seems they produced *King Lear* both ways—early on with the scene and later without it. Yet both versions are by Shakespeare. Both are his work. What happened? What caused this major change in the text? In my view, the earliest productions of the play revealed that the "trial" scene lengthened the time that Lear spent on the heath past the audience's endurance. Did Shakespeare, onstage or observing from the house, feel this waning of interest in the play's performance, and did he go back to the text and ruthlessly but professionally cut the scene?

Many modern directors (and editors) find the scene so compelling that they reinsert it. In doing this, there is neither right nor wrong, only choices to be made to meet the needs of a given production.

In fact, Shakespeare's revisions to his own work heighten our interest in it and gives us useful tools for understanding how he worked as a playwright. The very elasticity of the texts—the different versions that force us to study, think, and make choices—is one of the factors that keeps Shakespeare's work so alive for each new generation.

After Shakespeare died, when the company kept performing his works, changes for an individual performance would have been supervised by Heminges and Condell, the senior actors in the company. By then, however, the works had achieved a preferred shape, as reflected in the *First Folio.* The plays would have been published from the scripts held by the King's Men Company with the revisions that had worked best for the company over years of performance. This is why so many scholars prefer to base their quotations and interpretations on the *First Folio* versions of the plays.[121]

In school, Shakespeare's early training included altering, changing, turning texts; these exercises were a perfect fit for the realities of the theatrical world in London. His schoolboy experiences made him understand revision as necessary and creative. But what of the original act of writing the plays?

SHAKESPEARE WRITING IN PARTS

Shakespeare was constantly thinking of and searching for subjects for plays. While he was writing one, the seeds of others were germinating. After determining which play needed to be written immediately, he picked up his pen (in all probability the third or fourth quill from the left wing of a goose) and began to write.

---

121.   Jonathan Bate makes a strong statement as a First Folioist in his introduction to *Richard III.*

The most penetrating and original modern look at how Shakespeare wrote his plays is found in *Shakespeare in Parts,* by Simon Palfrey and Tiffany Stern. The authors insist on our recognizing that Shakespeare's mind was working on multiple levels as he wrote.

On the one hand, he envisioned his action unfolding as a totality, which would come to be represented by the script of the entire play. This he would give to the company; it would become the basis for the master or prompt script. On the other hand, Shakespeare knew that each actor would be given a "part book" containing just his character's lines, plus the three or four cueing words preceding them. Shakespeare would have to hold these different shapes in his mind as he wrote: how a given speech fit into the play as a whole, but also how each speech built the arc of the role of the individual character.

The history of the Lord Chamberlain's Men/Kings Men Company is one of remarkable stability over a period of more than thirty years. Shakespeare knew his actors intimately and wrote specifically for their strengths as performers. Conceiving his script was like putting together a complex puzzle, for its effectiveness was dependent on parts written for many individuals. Temperaments could wreak havoc with the process. Will Kempe, a founding member of the Lord Chamberlain's Men, was one of the great comic actors of the period, and the only one to leave the company except by retirement or death. Shortly after Kempe left, Shakespeare put into the mouth of Hamlet the lines

And let those that play

your clowns speak no more than is set down for them;

for there be of them that will themselves laugh, to

set on some quantity of barren spectators to laugh

too; though, in the mean time, some necessary

question of the play be then to be considered:

that's villainous...

Bottom, in *A Midsummer Night's Dream*, wants not only to direct everyone, but to play every part in the Pyramus and Thisbe play he and his friends are putting on to celebrate Duke Theseus's wedding. So Shakespeare revealed he was familiar with actors' egos. He had to write to satisfy the members of his company as well as himself.

Opera librettists and composers represent the closest parallel to this way of writing in modern times. According to Ann Thompson, author of the *Let's Go to the Opera* series,

"Singers were the first to be hired, either by the opera house management or the impresario who had to put the new season together. Composer and librettist, both low men on the totem pole, then had to provide those singers with music they liked and that observed all the perquisites of their status, such as she gets the first solo, he gets the last, that sort of thing. If she did not like a particular number, the soprano might pull one from her suitcase that she preferred, the so-called *aria di baule*, suitcase aria that might not even be by the composer in question. The number and difficulty of solos was most important during the Baroque era when indeed singers might demand half a dozen of them and reject them if they were not spectacular enough."

Of course this system produced hundreds of flawed, unsatisfying, patchwork operas. But it ultimately produced the great works of Rossini and Verdi as well. They needed to please the great singers who were necessary to bring their works to life.

In addition to his players, Shakespeare also had to keep in mind various structural considerations when designing his text, such as: to use or not use a prologue and epilogue; how to set up the cues;[122] which determinative event would come at the very center of the play, after which everything changed; what soliloquies came before or after this event; where to place songs artfully; how to contrast prose scenes or speeches in verse.

Some of these considerations would have been introduced to Shakespeare in his study of Plautus, Terence, and Seneca as a schoolboy; others grew with his practice and experience as a London professional. The constrictions of form and the challenges of performance fed and inspired his genius.

---

122.   Simon Palfrey and Tiffany Stern deal with this question in fascinating detail in *Shakespeare in Parts,* Sections II and III.

CONCLUSION

Despite the emphasis in the schools of Shakespeare's time on teaching Latin as a written and spoken language, the Elizabethan era was far more important for its astonishing development of English. The period actually marked the beginning of the end of the dominance of Latin over English.

The *King James Bible,* published in 1611, was the first English language work to reach what we would describe today as a mass audience. A team of fifty-four scholars had worked on it for seven years. During this period, Shakespeare was writing some of his most profound works: *Macbeth, Othello, Antony and Cleopatra, King Lear,* and *The Tempest* among them. To this day, the King James Bible and the *Complete Works of William Shakespeare* are without question the two most influential works in all of English literature.

The writers who dominated the Elizabethan and Jacobean era were all educated under the system described in this book. As students, they wrestled daily to combine two quite different linguistic systems. On the one hand were Latin and Greek, highly inflected and dependent on word endings for their syntax. On the other was English, which depended almost entirely upon word order to convey meaning.

Baldwin explains:

> One was thus forced to reduce his own language to its simplest order before he could transpose into or from

the Latin. The influence of the teaching of Latin upon the vernacular would, therefore, be double and opposite. On the one hand, in its simplest and fundamental form it would reduce the vernacular to its simplest and most direct order. This was the schoolboy stage. But as one grew in facility with the Latin or 'artificial' order, he would consciously or unconsciously imitate it in his vernacular. We thus have the divergent tendencies, already strongly marked in seventeenth century England, toward native simplicity of structure on the one hand, and Latin complication on the other.[123]

The richness of English in Shakespeare's time came not only from writers struggling to bring together two opposing linguistic systems. It came also from the energy triggered by an age of exploration and discovery which demanded, in response, an expanding world view and the imaginative means to express it. These imaginative means were found in the theatre, where the voices of great actors interpreted the words of great writers.

Thomas Heywood, an actor, playwright, and colleague of Shakespeare's wrote:

Our English tongue, which hath been the most harsh, uneven, and broken language of the world, part Dutch, part Irish, Saxon, Scotch, Welsh, and indeed a gallimaffry of many, but perfect in none, is now by this secondary means of playing continually refined, every writer striving in himself to add a new flourish unto it, so that in process, from the most rude and unpolite tongue, it is grown to a most perfect and composed language, and many excellent works, and elaborate poems writ in the same, that many nations grow inamored at our tongue (before despised).[124]

123.   Baldwin, *Shakspere's Small Latine and Lesse Greeke,* 1:585.
124.   Heywood, Pt 3.

Young William Shakespeare had had to work diligently on Latin throughout his years at grammar school. Somewhere along the way he fell in love with his own language. From then on he began not just to use his grammar school education, but to transcend it.

Educated in Latin, Shakespeare helped to form modern English. He put classic figures of speech to use in his own language. Inspired by exercises in Latin synonyms from his grammar school days and the encouragement to create neologisms (new words), he added hundreds of words to English: champion, circumstantial, cold-blooded, invulnerable, jaded, label, eyeball, fashionable, compromise, courtship, critic, dauntless, lackluster. His love of the language shines through in Thomas Mowbray's anguished reaction to banishment:

THOMAS MOWBRAY

A heavy sentence, my most sovereign liege...

The language I have learn'd these forty years,

My native English, now I must forego:

And now my tongue's use is to me no more

Than an unstringed viol or a harp,

Or like a cunning instrument cased up,

Or, being open, put into his hands

That knows no touch to tune the harmony:

Within my mouth you have engaol'd my tongue,

Doubly portcullis'd with my teeth and lips;

And dull unfeeling barren ignorance

Is made my gaoler to attend on me.

I am too old to fawn upon a nurse,

Too far in years to be a pupil now:

What is thy sentence then but speechless death,

Which robs my tongue from breathing native breath?...

Then thus I turn me from my country's light,

To dwell in solemn shades of endless night.

(*Richard II*, Act I Scene 3)

In the early 1590s, a siege of bubonic plague forced the closure of the London theatres. Shakespeare used this time to write and publish two epic poems, *Venus and Adonis* and *The Rape of Lucrece*. They were hugely popular. But in the year 1594, Shakespeare walked away from writing classics-based poetry to please educated and aristocratic courtiers, away from the entire literary world of the Elizabethan court over which he had triumphed. He went back to the theatre. What drew him? Acceptance? Belonging? Power? Perhaps it was because in the theatre he could create worlds of his own, put them onstage, and live in them. He could practice and struggle with an art form that constantly negotiated the border between reality and imagination—that in fact made imagination into reality. Above all, he could spend his energies creating worlds and people out of living, spoken language.

The perception of plays as literature came late to the Elizabethan-Jacobeans. When Ben Jonson published his *Complete Works* in 1616 he was ridiculed for including his plays. His insistence on their value stimulated literary interest in the plays of others and led to the publication of Shakespeare's *First Folio.* By then Shakespeare had died, and the Puritans had gained enough power to threaten the existence of the theatre. When his friends John Heminges and Henry Condell realized that Shakespeare's works could be lost forever, they edited and published them; we are in their debt. Thanks to them we can read and see and hear his plays today. We marvel at their continued expressiveness and relevance. How did Shakespeare do it? How could he have created such a body of work?

Other playwrights of the time had Shakespeare's education. Half of the playwrights working in London did not go to a university—they wrote with the skills they learned in grammar school. But none of them was Shakespeare. The content and form of what Shakespeare wrote had to do with his schooling, its depth came from the inexplicable gift of genius—possessing that, he needed no education past what he had found at the King Edward VI School in Stratford.

Shakespeare's Warwickshire contemporary, Fulke Greville, became the First Lord Brooke and Chancellor of the Exchequer. His secretary, claiming fitness for the position, once said: "And this I note, that though I were no graduate of the University, yet (by God's blessing) I had so much learning as fitted me for the places whereunto the Lord advanced me."[125]

---

125.   Willis, 99.

Shakespeare could have said the same as this humble man. It is a perfect description of Shakespeare's education and its affect on him. The place to which Shakespeare advanced was the theatre. And there both his learning and his genius fitted him.

AFTERWORD

Of the 800 schools established in a rush of idealism during the 16th and 17th centuries, only 100 still existed three generations later. The push of Henry VIII and his children to fill the educational vacuum Henry himself had created when he disolved the monasteries, and to increase and refocus education across the country, did not hold. And so this period in which the minds of Shakespeare and his contemporaries were trained was an anomaly, a century or so frozen in time, out of which would slowly develop the modern educational system in England.[126]

Fortunately for those of us eager to understand Shakespeare's schooling, educators of the sixteenth century wrote copiously of their theories and practices, including Erasmus, who helped establish the new curriculum that replaced the medieval system dominated by the philosophies of the Roman Catholic Church.

As we have seen, the book that dominated England's educational system in the 16th century and for three hundred years after was a Latin textbook, William Lily's *A Short Introduction of Grammar Generallie to be Used* (1557) commonly referred to as Lily's *Latin Grammar.* Johannes Susenbrotus's *Epitome troporum ac schematum et Grammaticorum & Rhetorume arte rhetorica libri tres* (1540), Richard Sherry's *A Treatise of Schemes and Tropes* (1550) and *A Treatise of the Figures of Grammer and Rhetorike* (1555), and Richard Mulcaster's, *The First Part*

---

126. See Jonathan Gathorne-Hardy's *The Old School Tie* for a complete history of the English public school system, honoring its complexity more than I can do in this book.

of the Elementerie (1582) are also important texts of the time and, thanks to the Internet, readily available to any modern researcher.

Roger Ascham, Elizabeth I's tutor, wrote of his methods in *The Scholemaster* (1570); Francis Clement described *The Petie Schole* (1587); Edmund Coote's *The English Schoolemaister* (1596) illustrated how slowly traditions and curricula changed; Leonard Culman's *Sententiae Pueriles* (1612) was one of the ubiquitous texts of the day; John Brinsley gave much detailed advice on teaching in *Ludus Literarius: or, The Grammar Schoole* (1612) and *Pueriles Confabulatiunculae* (1617); while Charles Hoole's *A New Discovery of the Old Art of Teaching Schoole* (1660) made specific which books were used at each grade level (or form) and how lessons were presented from Shakespeare's time on into the next century.

Researchers have pored over each line of Shakespeare's plays and poems looking for connections to the literature of his time. Here we include among others Sister Miriam Joseph's *Shakespeare's Use of Language*, Richmond Noble's *Shakespeare's Biblical Knowledge*, Steven Marx's *Shakespeare and the Bible*, Virgil K. Whitaker's *Shakespeare's Use of Learning*, and H.E.D. Anders' thesis on *Shakespeare's Books*.

This book, *Shakespeare's Education*, is far from comprehensive. It is an overview. For the reader seeking a starting point, it succeeds, I hope, in establishing the main patterns of his schooling and in connecting these to his writing. But there is much, much archival material—correspondence, school statutes, public records—that awaits serious scholars wanting to explore this subject in greater depth.

APPENDIX A

BRINSLEY TEACHES VERSIFICATION

Brinsley continues his instruction in versification. Speaking of students he asks:

1. That they be expert in scanning a verse and in proving every quantity, according to their rules, and so use to practice in their lectures daily. To keep them that they shall never bodge in their entrance... but to enter with ease, certainty and delight... making sure that your scholars know not the verses aforehand... dictate unto them as you did in prose. Cause also so many as you would have to learn together, to set down the English as you dictate. Secondly... to write down all the words in Latin *verbatim*, or Grammatically. Thirdly, having just the same words, let them try which of them can soonest turn them into the order of a verse:... And then lastly, read thee over the verse of Ovid, that they may see that themselves have made the very same; or wherein they missed, this shall much encourage and assure them....

2. Cause them to turn the verses of their lecture into other verses... yet ever to keep the very phrase of the Poet, there or in other places, only transposing the words or phrase, or changing some words or phrase, or the numbers, or persons, or applying them to matters which are familiar, as they did in imitating *Epistles*. This may be practiced... either being given at eleven to be brought at one, or at evening to be brought in the morning, or both.

3. As they proceed, to cause them to contrast their lectures, drawing seven or eight verses into four or five, or fewer; yet still laboring to express the whole

matter of their Author in their own verse, and every circumstance with all significant Metaphors, and other tropes and phrases, so much as they can. Thus they may proceed if you will... contracting a certain number, as some five or six a day... striving who can express their Author most lively.

4. Moreover, that your scholars may be able to write verses *extempore*, of any ordinary Theme... By this practice kept duely, to make some such verses twice in the day (as to give them Themes before their breaking up at noon, to bring them at one of the clock, and at night to bring them in the morning, or nine, as before...) or... before they are to play, to versify of some Theme not thought of... you shall find that they will grow in so good sort, as shall be requisite to make you verses, *extempore* of any usual Theme, without hindering of their other studies... This exercise is very commendable... for that it is a very great sharpener of the wit, as was said, and a stirrer up of invention... In this matter of versifying... I take this Imitation of the most excellent patterns to be the surest rule.[127]

---

127.   Brinsley, *The Grammar School,* 193-95.

APPENDIX B

TWO KINDLY SCHOOLMASTERS: HOLOFERNES AND SIR HUGH EVANS

In about 1592 or 1593 Shakespeare wrote a lively, charming, but most definitely intellectual comedy which he called *Love's Labour's Lost*. Its audience was not the apprentices and popular crowd that filled the Theatre and the Curtain but far more likely the young aristocrats inhabiting the Inns of Court (a popular performance venue for plays of the time) and in particular Henry Wriothesley, the Earl of Southampton, who had rewarded Shakespeare handsomely for writing the epic poems *Venus and Adonis* and *The Rape of Lucrece*. Almost as if to prove his superiority to the small town middle class from which he came, and to identify himself with the young students at the Inns of Court who were there to learn enough law to manage the great estates they would eventually inherit, Shakespeare made four such young men the leading characters in his play. In the fourth act he introduces two intellectual figures, Holofernes the schoolmaster and Nathaniel the curate, through whom he could make fun of the pedantry of the time.

Happy, wistful, nostalgic, and excessively pedantic Holofernes seeks out his friend Nathaniel and sings praises of learning in English and Latin. The brilliant young men at the Inns of Court would catch each classical allusion and every Latinate turn (or *mis*turn) of phrase.

In *Love's Labour's Lost* Act 4 Scene 2, Holofernes, Sir Nathaniel and Dull enter discussing the hunting of a deer. Immediately Holofernes uses Latin words to demonstrate his learning; and enjoys extending thoughts with synonyms—one of the figures of speech so diligently practiced in the Elizabethan schoolroom. He will go on to demonstrate alliteration, epithets, anaphora (repetition of the same word to begin a series—here the repetition of 'un-'), apostrophe, metaphor, personification and other verbal usages which his audience would instantly recognize.

SIR NATHANIEL

[Describing the Day the Princess has spent hunting, he says: the Princess has had]

Very reverend sport, truly; and done in the testimony

of a good conscience.

HOLOFERNES

The deer was, as you know, sanguis, in blood; ripe

as the pomewater (*large apple*), who now hangeth like a jewel in the ear of caelo, the sky, the welkin, the heaven;

and anon falleth like a crab on the face of terra,

the soil, the land, the earth.

SIR NATHANIEL

Truly, Master Holofernes, the epithets are sweetly

varied, like a scholar at the least: but, sir, I assure ye, it was a buck of the first head (in its fifth year with a full head of antlers).

HOLOFERNES

Sir Nathaniel, haud credo. (*Latin for I can't believe it*)

DULL

'Twas not a haud credo; (*Dull hears haud credo as old grey doe*) 'twas a pricket (*a deer in its second year*)

HOLOFERNES

Most barbarous intimation! yet a kind of

insinuation, as it were, in via, in way, of

explication; facere (*to make*), as it were, replication, or

rather, *ostentare*, to show, as it were, his

inclination, after his undressed, unpolished,

uneducated, unpruned, untrained, or rather,

unlettered, or ratherest, unconfirmed fashion, to

insert again my haud credo for a deer.

DULL

I said the deer was not a haud credo; twas a pricket.

HOLOFERNES

Twice-sod (*twice-boiled*) simplicity, his coctus! (*twice-boiled in Latin*)

O thou monster Ignorance, how deformed dost thou look!

SIR NATHANIEL

Sir, he hath never fed of the dainties that are bred

in a book; he hath not eat paper, as it were; he

hath not drunk ink: his intellect is not

replenished; he is only an animal, only sensible in

the duller parts:

And such barren plants are set before us, that we

thankful should be,

Which we of taste and feeling are, for those parts that

do fructify in us more than he.

For as it would ill become me to be vain, indiscreet, or a fool,

So were there a patch set on learning, to see him in a school:

But omne bene, say I; being of an old father's mind,

Many can brook the weather that love not the wind.

DULL

You two are book-men...

HOLOFERNES

Sir Nathaniel, will you hear an extemporal epitaph

on the death of the deer? And, to humour the

ignorant, call I the deer the princess killed a pricket.

SIR NATHANIEL

Perge (*Latin for 'go on'*), good Master Holofernes, perge; so
it shall

please you to abrogate scurrility.

HOLOFERNES

I will something affect the letter, for it argues facility.

The preyful princess pierced and prick'd a pretty

pleasing pricket;

Some say a sore (*a buck in its fourth year*); but not a sore,
till now made

sore with shooting.

The dogs did yell: put L to sore, then sorel (*a buck in its third year*) jumps

from thicket;

Or pricket sore, or else sorel; the people fall a-hooting.

If sore be sore, then L (*the roman numeral for 50*) to sore makes fifty sores one sorel.

Of one sore I an hundred make by adding but one more L.

SIR NATHANIEL

A rare talent!...

HOLOFERNES

This is a gift that I have, simple, simple; a

foolish extravagant spirit, full of forms, figures,

shapes, objects, ideas, apprehensions, motions,

revolutions: these are begot in the ventricle of

memory, nourished in the womb of *pia mater*, and

delivered upon the mellowing of occasion. But the

gift is good in those in whom it is acute, and I am

thankful for it.

Here we can see Shakespeare making fun of himself, for surely this "foolish, extravagant spirit, full of forms, figures, shapes, objects, ideas" is a description of his own facility. The scene continues to allude to Shakespeare's education. Nathaniel refers to the education of women in his next speech:

> SIR NATHANIEL
>
> Sir, I praise the Lord for you; and so may my
>
> parishioners; for their sons are well tutored by
>
> you, and their daughters profit very greatly under
>
> you: you are a good member of the commonwealth.

> HOLOFERNES
>
> Mehercle, if their sons be ingenuous, they shall
>
> want no instruction; if their daughters be capable,
>
> I will put it to them: but *vir sapit qui pauca*
>
> *Loquitur (a man is wise who says little)*; a soul feminine saluteth us.

As the "soul feminine" approaches, Holofernes talks of Mantuan, one of the most studied Latin authors,

> Ah, good old Mantuan! I
>
> may speak of thee as the traveller doth of Venice;
>
> *Venetia, Venetia,*
>
> *Chi non ti vede non ti pretia.*

Old Mantuan, old Mantuan! who understandeth thee

not, loves thee not. Ut, re, sol, la, mi, fa.

Under pardon, sir, what are the contents? or rather,

as Horace says in his--What, my soul, verses?

The "soul feminine" is a woman, Jaquenetta, who brings a letter for them to read to her. The letter is in verse – a welcome chance for Holofernes to critique its style.

SIR NATHANIEL

Ay, sir, and very learned.

HOLOFERNES

Let me hear a staff, a stanze, a verse; lege, domine.

You find not the apostraphas, and so miss the

accent: let me supervise the canzonet...

I do dine to-day at the father's of a certain pupil

of mine; where, if, before repast, it shall please

you to gratify the table with a grace, I will, on my

privilege I have with the parents of the foresaid

child or pupil, undertake your *ben venuto*; where I

will prove those verses to be very unlearned,

neither savouring of poetry, wit, nor invention: I

beseech your society.

SIR NATHANIEL

And thank you too; for society, saith the text, is

the happiness of life.

HOLOFERNES

Away! the gentles are at

their game, and we will to our recreation.

Closer, probably, to the more down-home masters he knew in Stratford is Sir Hugh Evans, the charming schoolmaster in *The Merry Wives of Windsor.* Sir Hugh's dialogue is written with a strong Welsh accent, and since Shakespeare's teacher Jenkins had a Welsh name scholars are tempted to suggest that Sir Hugh Evans is a portrait of Jenkins. But Jenkins, Welsh name aside, was born and brought up a Londoner so Hugh Evans may be a pure creation of Shakespeare's imagination. The fourth act of the play opens with a scene which seems to have little purpose other than to be a vaudeville style sketch satirizing the education system of the day. Though I've seen no remark on it, when Sir Hugh (a title which shows he has a B.A. degree) says "Master Slender is let the boys leave to play," it suggests that Slender (a relative of the dotty Judge

Shallow) was Sir Hugh's assistant at the school, the usher who would have had charge of the younger boys. There are several woodcuts that show scenes of schoolrooms, one of which has a single boy standing in front of a teacher ensconced behind a high desk.[128] The boy must be the one at the moment called forth to be questioned by the teacher as we see Sir Hugh questioning William Page. Mistress Page indicates that parents then as now were eager to keep tabs on their children's performance at school.

SCENE I. A street.

MISTRESS PAGE, MISTRESS QUICKLY and WILLIAM PAGE encountering SIR HUGH EVANS

MISTRESS PAGE

How now, Sir Hugh! no school to-day?

SIR HUGH EVANS

No; Master Slender is let the boys leave to play.

MISTRESS QUICKLY

Blessing of his heart!

MISTRESS PAGE

---

128.   Riggs, 26.

Sir Hugh, my husband says my son profits nothing in world at his book. I pray you, ask him some questions in his accidence. *(The grammar book of the younger boys)*

SIR HUGH EVANS

Come hither, William; hold up your head; come.

MISTRESS PAGE

Come on, sirrah; hold up your head; answer your master, be not afraid.

SIR HUGH EVANS

William, how many numbers is in nouns?

WILLIAM PAGE

Two.

MISTRESS QUICKLY

Truly, I thought there had been one number more, because they say, "Od's nouns." *(a confusion with God's wounds!, a common exclamation. She's hearing the need for three, an odd number)*

SIR HUGH EVANS

Peace your tattlings! What is 'fair,' William? *(asking for the Latin translation)*

WILLIAM PAGE

Pulcher.

MISTRESS QUICKLY

Polecats! there are fairer things than polecats, sure.

SIR HUGH EVANS

You are a very simplicity 'oman: I pray you peace.

What is 'lapis,' William?

WILLIAM PAGE

A stone.

SIR HUGH EVANS

And what is 'a stone,' William?

WILLIAM PAGE

A pebble. *(William mistakenly gives a synonym when a "turn" back to Latin is required.)*

SIR HUGH EVANS

No, it is 'lapis:' I pray you, remember in your prain. *(Substituting ' p' for 'b' is typical of a Welsh accent.)*

WILLIAM PAGE

Lapis.

SIR HUGH EVANS

That is a good William. What is he, William, that does lend articles?

WILLIAM PAGE

Articles are borrowed of the pronoun, and be thus declined, Singulariter, nominativo, hic, haec, hoc.

SIR HUGH EVANS

Nominativo, hig, hag, hog; pray you, mark: *('g' substitutes for a 'k' sound in a Welsh accent)* genitivo, hujus. Well, what is your accusative case?

WILLIAM PAGE

Accusativo, hinc.

SIR HUGH EVANS

I pray you, have your remembrance, child, accusative, hung, hang, hog.

MISTRESS QUICKLY

'Hang-hog' is Latin for bacon, I warrant you.

SIR HUGH EVANS

Leave your prabbles, 'oman. What is the focative *('f' for 'v' – another Welsh characteristic)* case, William?

WILLIAM PAGE

O,--vocativo, O.

SIR HUGH EVANS

Remember, William; focative is caret.

MISTRESS QUICKLY

And that's a good root.

SIR HUGH EVANS

'Oman, forbear.

MISTRESS PAGE

Peace!

SIR HUGH EVANS

What is your genitive case plural, William?

WILLIAM PAGE

Genitive case!

SIR HUGH EVANS

Ay.

WILLIAM PAGE

Genitive,--horum, harum, horum.

MISTRESS QUICKLY

Vengeance of Jenny's case! fie on her! never name her, child,
if she be a whore.

SIR HUGH EVANS

For shame, 'oman.

MISTRESS QUICKLY

You do ill to teach the child such words: he teaches him to hick and to hack *(the famous Dr. Simon Forman was not above seducing his women patients, and noted in his diaries whether or not they were willing to 'halek.' This would seem to relate to Mistress Quickly's 'hick' and 'hack')*, which they'll do fast enough of themselves, and to call 'horum:' fie upon you!

SIR HUGH EVANS

'Oman, art thou lunatics? hast thou no understandings for thy cases and the numbers of the genders? Thou art as foolish Christian creatures as I would desires.

MISTRESS PAGE

Prithee, hold thy peace.

SIR HUGH EVANS

Show me now, William, some declensions of your pronouns.

WILLIAM PAGE

Forsooth, I have forgot.

SIR HUGH EVANS

It is qui, quae, quod: if you forget your 'quies,' your 'quaes,' and your 'quods,' you must be preeches. Go your ways, and play; go. *('breeches' meaning whipped, but it seems a mild and gentle threat. Sir Hugh saves his anger for the uneducated Mistress Quickly, as he seems eager to let William go play.)*

MISTRESS PAGE

He is a better scholar than I thought he was.

SIR HUGH EVANS

He is a good sprag *(spritely)* memory. Farewell, Mistress Page.

MISTRESS PAGE

Adieu, good Sir Hugh.

Exit SIR HUGH EVANS

Get you home, boy. Come, we stay too long.

One can see Sir Hugh and William taking a bow and exiting to applause, as everyone in the theatre would have relived his schoolboy days through this little scene.

APPENDIX C

IMITATION: PLUTARCH, PORTIA, AND CLEOPATRA

However it was meted out, the basic principle of Tudor education was imitation, and its practice trained Shakespeare in his playwriting. Plutarch's *Lives of the Noble Grecians and Romans* as translated from the French version of James Amyot by Sir Thomas North was published first in 1579, and reissued in 1595. This was the version on which Shakespeare based his classical history plays.

From Marcus Brutus in Plutarch's *Lives*

> His wife Porcia... was the daughter of Cato, whom Brutus married... .This young lady being excellently well seen in philosophy.... loving her husband well, and being of a noble courage as she was also wise, because she would not ask her husband what he ailed before she had made some proof by herself, she took a little razor such as barbers occupy to pare men's nails; and causing all her maids and women to go out of her chamber, gave herself a great gash withal in her thigh, that she was straight all of a gore blood...

> Then, perceiving her husband was marvelously out of quiet and that he could take no rest, even in her greatest pain of all she spake in this sort unto him: "I being, O Brutus," said she, "the daughter of Cato, was married unto thee, not to be thy bedfellow and companion in bed and at board only, like a harlot; but to be partaker also with thee of they good and evil fortune. Now for thyself, I can find no cause of fault in thee touching our match; but for my part, how may I show my duty towards thee, and how much I would do for thy sake, if I cannot constantly bear a secret mischance

or grief with thee, which requireth secrecy and fidelity? I confess that a woman's wit commonly is too weak to keep a secret safely; but yet, Brutus, good education and the company of virtuous men have some power to reform the defect of nature. And for myself, I have this benefit moreover, that I am the daughter of Cato and wife of Brutus. This notwithstanding, I did not trust to any of these things before, until that now I have found by experience, that no pain nor grief whatsoever can overcome me." With these words she showed him her wound on her thigh and told him what she had done to prove herself. Brutus was amazed to hear what she said unto him, and lifting up his hands to heaven, he besought the gods to give him the grace he might bring his enterprise to so good pass, that he might be found a husband worthy of so noble a wife as Porcia; so he then did comfort her the best he could.

Shakespeare took this passage, "turned" it, as he had practiced so often in the Stratford Grammar School, changing phrases from one language into another, and finally versifying it: changing it from prose into verse.

Portia:

You've ungently, Brutus,

Stole from my bed: and yesternight at supper

You suddenly arose and walked about,

Musing and sighing, with your arms across;

And when I asked you what the matter was,

You stared upon me with ungentle looks;

I urged you further: then you scratched your head

And too impatiently stamped with your foot:

Yet I insisted, yet you answered not,

But with a angry wafture of your hand

Gave sign for me to leave you: so I did,

Fearing to strengthen that impatience

Which seemed too much enkindled, and withal

Hoping it was but an effect of humour,

Which sometime hath his hour with every man.

It will not let you eat, nor talk, nor sleep,

And could it work so much upon your shape

As it hath much prevailed on your condition,

I should not know you, Brutus. Dear my lord,

Make me acquainted with your cause of grief...

Within the bond of marriage, tell me, Brutus,

Is it excepted I should know no secrets

That appertain to you? Am I your self

But, as it were, in sort or limitation,

To keep with you at meals, comfort your bed,

And talk to you sometimes? Dwell I but in the suburbs

Of your good pleasure? If it be no more

Portia is Brutus' harlot, not his wife...

I grant I am a woman, but withal

A woman that Lord Brutus took to wife:

I grant I am a woman, but withal

A woman well reputed, Cato's daughter.

Think you I am no stronger than my sex,

Being so fathered and so husbanded?

Tell me your counsels, I will not disclose 'em:

I have made strong proof of my constancy,

Giving myself a voluntary wound

Here in the thigh: can I bear that with patience

And not my husband's secrets?

Brutus:

      O ye gods,

Render me worthy of t his noble wife.

Hark, hark! One knocks: Portia, go in awhile;

By and by thy bosom shall partake

The secrets of my heart:

All my engagements I will construe to thee,

All the charactery of my sad brows...

In the biography of Mark Antonio, Plutarch describes the wonderful sumptuousness of Cleopatra, Queen of Egypt, going unto Antonius:

... she disdained to set forward otherwise but to take her barge in the river of Cydnus, the poop whereof was of gold, the sails of purple, and the oars of silver; which kept stroke in rowing after the sound of the music of flutes, hautboys, citherns, viols, and such other instruments as they played upon in the barge. And now for the person of herself: she was laid under a pavilion of cloth of gold of tissue, appareled and attired like the goddess Venus... and hard by her on either hand of her, pretty fair boys appareled as painters do set forth god Cupid, with little fans in their hands, with the which they fanned wind upon her.

And Shakespeare (who surely must have been recognized at school as good at "turning") versified this in a famous speech of Enobarbus in *Antony and Cleopatra* (Act II Scene 2):

Enobarbus:

When she first met Mark Antony, she pursed up his heart, upon the river of Cydnus...

The barge she sat in, like a burnisht throne

Burned upon the water: the poop was beaten gold;

Purple the sails, and so perfumed that

The winds were love-sick with them; the oars were silver,

Which to the tune of flutes kept stroke and made

The water which they beat to follow faster,

As amorous of their strokes. For her own person,

It beggared all description, she did lie

In her pavilion, cloth-of-gold, of tissue,

O'er picturing that Venus where we see

The fancy outwork nature: on each side her

Stood pretty dimpled boys, like smiling Cupids,

With divers-coloured fans, whose wind did seem

To glow the delicate cheeks which they did cool...

APPENDIX D

ADAPTATION: OVID AND *A MIDSUMMER NIGHT'S DREAM*

Shakespeare and his contemporaries referred often to the Roman poet Ovid, whose *Metamorphoses* retold the great classical myths. It was a favorite source for Shakespeare. He used it most directly and fully in the epic poems *Venus and Adonis* and (with other sources) *The Rape of Lucrece,* and comedically in his transposition of Ovid's *Pyramus and Thisbe* into the play within a play in *A Midsummer Night's Dream.* The Golding translation of 1567 was readily available to Shakespeare, though his schooldays would have acquainted him deeply with the original as well.

Golding uses the (by Shakespeare's time) old fashioned, jingly, and highly rhythmic "fourteener," a seven-foot iambic line that easily breaks into four- and three-foot jingly phrases. These are comically emphasized by Bottom (as Pyramus) and Flute (as Thisbe) in Shakespeare's version of their tragic tale.

Compare Ovid's poem to the fifth act of *A Midsummer Night's Dream.*

OVID'S VERSION

PYRAMUS AND THISBE— translated by Golding[129]

Within the town (of whose huge walls so monstrous high and thick
The fame is given Semiramis for making them of brick)
Dwelt hard together two young folk in houses joined so near
That under all one roof well nigh both twain conveyed were.

The name of him was Pyramus, and Thisbe called was she.
So fair a man in all the East was none alive as he,
Nor ne'er a woman, maid, nor wife in beauty like to her.
This neighbrod *(neighborhood)* bred acquaintance first, this neighbrod first did stir
The secret sparks, this neighbrod first an entrance in did show,
For love to come to that to which it afterward did grow.
And if that right had taken place, they had been man and wife,
But still their Parents went about to let *(separate)* which (for their life)
They could not let. For both their hearts with equal flame did burn.
No man was privy to their thoughts. And for to serve their turn
Instead of talk they used signs.   The closelier they suppressed
The fire of love, the fiercer still it raged in their breast.

The wall that parted house from house had riven therein a cranny

---

Which shrunk at making of the wall. This fault not marked of any
Of many hundred years before (what doth not love espy?)
These lovers first of all found out, and made a way whereby
To talk together secretly, and through the same did go
Their loving whisperings very light and safely to and fro.
Now as at one side Pyramus and Thisbe on the other
Stood often drawing one of them the pleasant breath from other,
"O thou envious wall," they said, "Why let'st thou lovers thus?
What matter were it if that thou permitted both of us
In arms each other to embrace? Or if thou think that this
Were overmuch, yet mightest thou at least make room to kiss.
And yet thou shalt not find us churls: we think ourselves in debt
For the same piece of courtesy, in vouching safe to let
Our sayings to our friendly ears thus freely come and go."
Thus having where they stood in vain complained of their woe,
When night drew near, they bad adieu and each gave kisses sweet
Unto the paget on their side, the which did never meet.

Next Morning with her cheerful light had driven the stars aside
And Phoebus with his burning beams the dewy grass had dried.
These lovers at their wonted place by foreappointment met
Where after much complaint and more they convenanted to get
Away from such as watched them, and in the Evening late
To steal out of their fathers house and eke the city gate.

And to the intent that in the fields they strayed not up and down,
They did agree at Ninus Tomb to meet without the town
And tarry underneath a tree that by the same did grow

Which was a fair high Mulberry with fruit as white as snow,
Hard by a cool and trickling spring. This bargain pleased
them both.

And so daylight (which to their thought away but slowly
goeth)
Did in the Ocean fall to rest: and night from thence doth rise.
As soon as darkness once was come, straight Thisbe did
devise
A shift to wend her out of doors, that none that were within
Perceived her: and mussing her with clothes about her chin,
That no man might discern her face, to Ninus tomb she came
Unto the tree, and sat her down there underneath the same.

Love made her bold.   But see the chance, there comes
besmeared with blood
About the chaps a Lioness all foaming from the wood,
From slaughter lately made of kine, to staunch her bloody
thirst
With water of the foresaid spring. Whom Thisbe spying first
Afar by moonlight, thereupon with fearful steps gan fly,
And in a dark and irksome cave did hide herself thereby.

And as she fled away for haste she let her mantle fall
The which for fear she left behind, not looking back at all.
Now when the cruel Lioness her thirst had stanched well,
In going to the wood she found the slender weed that fell
From Thisbe, which with bloody teeth in pieces she did tear.

The night was somewhat further spent ere Pyramus came
there:
Who, seeing in this subtle sand the print of Lion's paw
Waxed pale for fear. But when also the bloody cloak he saw
All rent and torn, "One night," he said, "Shall lovers two
confound,
Of which long life deserved she of all that live on ground.
My soul deserves of this mischance the peril for to bear.
I wretch have been the death of thee, which to this place of
fear

Did cause thee in the night to come, and came not here
before.
My wicked limbs and wretched guts with cruel teeth
therefore
Devour ye, oh ye Lions all that in this rock do dwell.
But Cowards use to wish for death"

The slender weed that fell
From Thisbe up he takes, and straight doth bear it to the
tree,
Which was appointed erst the place of meeting for to be.
And when he had bewept and kissed the garment which he
knew,
"Receive thou my blood, too!" quoth he, and therewithal he
drew
His sword, the which among his guts he thrust, and by and
by
Did draw it from the bleeding wound binning for to die
And cast himself upon his back

The blood did spin on high
As when a conduit pipe is cracked, the water bursting out
Doth shoot itself a great way off and pierce the air about.
The leaves that were upon the tree besprinkled with his
blood
Were dyed black. The root also bestained as it stood
A deep dark purple color straight upon the berries cast.

Anon scarce ridded of her fear with which she was aghast,
For doubt of disappointing him, comes Thisbe forth in haste,
And for her lover looks about rejoicing for to tell
How hardly she had scaped that night the danger that befell.
And as she knew right well the place and fashion of the tree
(As which she saw so late before) even so when she did see
The color of the berries turned, she was uncertain whether
It were the tree at which they both agreed to meet together.

While in this doubtful stound she stood, she cast her eye
aside

And there beweltered in his blood her lover she espied
Lie sprawling with his dying limbs: at which she started back,
And looked pale as any Box, a shuddering through her struck
Even like the Sea which suddenly with whishing noise doth move,
When with a little blast of wind it is but touched above.
But when approaching nearer him she knew it was her love,
She beat her breast, she shrieked out, she tare her golden hairs,
And taking him between her arms did wash his wounds with tears.
She meant her weeping with his blood, and kissing all his face
(Which now became as cold as ice) she cried in woeful case
"Alas what chance my Pyramus hath parted thee and me?
Make answer, O my Pyramus, It is thy Thisb, e'en she
Whom thou dost love most heartily that speaketh unto thee.
Give care and raise thy heavy head,"
He, hearing Thisbe's name,
Lift up his dying eyes, and having seen her close the same.
But when she knew her mantle there and saw his scabbard lie
Without the sword: "Unhappy man, thy love hath made thee die:
Thy love," she said, "Hath made thee slay thyself. This hand of mine
Is strong enough to do the like. My love no less than thine
Shall give me force to work my wound. I will pursue the dead.
And wretched woman as I am, it shall of me be said
That like as of thy death I was the only cause and blame,
So am I thy companion eke and partner in the same.
For death which only could alas asunder part us twain,
Shall never so dissever us but we will meet again.
And you the Parents of us both, most wretched folk alive
Let this request that I shall make in both our names bylive,
Entreat you to permit that we whom chaste and steadfast love

And whom even death hath joined in one, may as it doth behove
In one grave be together laid. And thou unhappy tree
Which shroudest now the corpse of one, and shalt anon thorugh me
Shroud two, of this same slaughter hold the sicker signs for ay.
Black be the color of thy fruit and mourning like always,
Such as the murder of us twain may evermore bewray."

This said, she took the sword yet warm with slaughter of her love
And setting it beneath her breast, did to her heart it shove.

Her prayer with the Gods and with their Parents took effect.
For when the fruit is thoroughly ripe, the berry is bespect
With color tending to a black. And that which after fire
Remained, rested in one tomb, as Thisbe did desire.

APPENDIX E

HOTSPUR AND THE PRISONERS: AN EXERCISE IN *CHREIA*

Hotspur's tale about why he wants to keep his prisoners is, like Cassius's speech in *Julius Caesar,* an extended exercise in Aphthonius's *Chreia:*

HOTSPUR

My liege, I did deny no prisoners.
laudativus

But I remember, when the fight was done,

When I was dry with rage and extreme toil,

Breathless and faint, leaning upon my sword,
laudativus

Came there a certain lord, neat, and trimly dress'd,

Fresh as a bridegroom; and his chin new reap'd

Show'd like a stubble-land at harvest-home;

He was perfumed like a milliner;
contrarium

And 'twixt his finger and his thumb he held

A pouncet-box, which ever and anon

He gave his nose and took't away again;

Who therewith angry, when it next came there,
exemplum

Took it in snuff; and still he smiled and talk'd,

And as the soldiers bore dead bodies by,

He call'd them untaught knaves, unmannerly,
causa

To bring a slovenly unhandsome corse

Betwixt the wind and his nobility.

With many holiday and lady terms

He question'd me; amongst the rest, demanded
causa

My prisoners in your majesty's behalf.

I then, all smarting with my wounds being cold,
parabola

To be so pester'd with a popinjay,

Out of my grief and my impatience,
parabola

Answer'd neglectingly I know not what,

He should or he should not; for he made me mad

To see him shine so brisk and smell so sweet
contrarium

And talk so like a waiting-gentlewoman

Of guns and drums and wounds,—God save the mark! —
causa

And telling me the sovereign'st thing on earth

Was parmaceti for an inward bruise;
testamonium

And that it was great pity, so it was,
veterum

This villanous salt-petre should be digg'd

Out of the bowels of the harmless earth,

Which many a good tall fellow had destroy'd

So cowardly; and but for these vile guns,

He would himself have been a soldier.
exemplum

This bald unjointed chat of his, my lord,

I answer'd indirectly, as I said;
causa

And I beseech you, let not his report
brevis epilogus

Come current for an accusation

Betwixt my love and your high majesty.

Henry IV Part 1 Act 1 scene 2

This, like Cassius's speech, shows Shakespeare did not invent the oratorical structures in his plays, rather he applied techniques learned and practiced in school.

APPENDIX F

THE EDUCATION OF THREE OF SHAKESPEARE'S CONTEMPORARIES

Shakespeare and his great colleagues Thomas Kyd, Christopher Marlowe, and Ben Jonson lived in widely separated towns, but their destiny—writing plays in London—and the education they drew upon were in essence the same.

THOMAS KYD

Kyd was born in 1558, a poor child in London, son of a scrivener or professional scribe. He had the luck to attend the famous Merchant Taylors' School, founded by that guild.[130] Its first headmaster Richard Mulcaster was one of the many passionate and vocal educational theorists of the time. Born in 1530/31 (and so about the age of Shakespeare's father) Mulcaster was educated at Eton, Cambridge, and Oxford. He dared to advocate the continuation of teaching and writing in English as well as in the prescribed Latin. His fame rests on two books: *Positions Concerning the Training Up of Children* (1581) and *The First Part of the Elementarie* (1582). His recommendations for education sound extraordinarily modern for he advocated university training for teachers, not unlike that for doctors

---

130.   In his book *Shakespeare the Boy,* 106, William J. Rolfe says Merchant Taylors' school was founded as a feeder or preparatory school for St. John's College, Oxford. This would suggest that aristocratic boys as well as boys from the middle class might be its students. Mulcaster advocated teaching English as well as Latin. In *The Old School Tie,* Jonathan Gathorne-Hardy emphasizes how many of the schools established in Shakespeare's time were founded by the liveried companies, i.e., the trade guilds (26).

or lawyers and careful selection of teachers attracted by good salaries. He would assign the best teachers to the lowest grades and he believed (as we do now) in a close association between teachers and parents. He emphasized the importance of individual differences in children, and he wanted a curriculum adjusted to these differences. Readiness, he felt, rather than age should determine a child's progress.

From Mulcaster, students received an unusually sophisticated exposure to the theatre. Sir James Whitlocke,[131] who came to the school in 1575, remembers: "I was brought up at school under Mr. Mulcaster, in the famous school of the Merchant Taylors in London... Yearly he presented some plays to the court, in which his scholars were [the] only actors, and I one among them, and by that means [he] taught...good behavior and audacity."

When Shakespeare was writing his first plays in London, Kyd's *The Spanish Tragedy* (written about 1589) was playing to acclaim. The prototypical revenge tragedy, it was enormously popular and hugely influential. Shakespeare himself was not untouched by the success of this play. But there was an additional Kyd/Shakespeare connection in that Kyd is thought by some to have written an early version of *Hamlet* used by Shakespeare as the basis for his great tragedy. Revenge tragedies, so popular with Elizabethan audiences, were based on the Senecan tragedies studied by most boys at grammar school and drawn upon by Kyd, Shakespeare, and all contemporary tragedians.

---

131.   John Taplin, author of *Shakespeare's Country Families*, notes that Sir James Whitlocke married Elizabeth Balstrode, a progenator of Thomas Nash. This young man married Shakespeare's granddaughter.

CHRISTOPHER MARLOWE

Later, in his playwriting years, Thomas Kyd (to his detriment) became a close friend and roommate of Christopher Marlowe—atheist, spy, reprobate, and playwright. The influence of Christopher Marlowe on the works of Shakespeare is powerful: Marlowe's lines are quoted in *As You Like It* and in *The Merry Wives of Windsor*; it is hard to read *The Merchant of Venice* without acknowledging Marlowe's prior *Jew of Malta,* or to read Shakespeare's *Richard II* without connecting it to Marlowe's *Edward II.* The fact that Marlowe was writing *Hero and Leander* at the same time Shakespeare was writing *Venus and Adonis* and *The Rape of Lucrece,* and the thought that he hoped to attract the Earl of Southampton as a patron, give weight to the theory that Marlowe was the rival poet in Shakespeare's *Sonnets.* More important, responding to powerful influences like Marlowe's was a crucial element in how Shakespeare learned to write his plays.

The son of a Canterbury shoemaker, Christopher Marlowe was six years younger than Thomas Kyd and so was beginning his education in Canterbury as Kyd was leaving Merchant Taylors'. Marlowe's first school is unknown but for at least two years he had a scholarship of four pounds a year at King's School in Canterbury (1579-80).[132] Before this, because his father was poor, he might have attended the free school recently established across the street from Canterbury's Eastbridge Hospital. Like Merchant Taylors', as part of the rigorous curriculum, King's put on plays— in this case plays for Christmas holidays. The experience stayed in Marlowe's mind, for several years later (1584-

---

132.   *Oxford Dictionary of National Biography,* Marlowe.

85), when he was twenty, his earliest play was written for a group of child actors.[133]

From King's, Marlowe was recommended for an Archbishop Parker scholarship to Cambridge University. As one of fifty scholarship recipients "both destitute of the help of friends and endowed with minds apt for learning,"[134] Marlowe went to Cambridge where he earned both a BA and an MA, the only one of our trio to have a university education. At the end of his masterful essay on Marlowe for the 1911 *Encyclopedia Britannica,* the poet Charles Swinburne says: "He is the greatest discoverer, the most daring and inspired pioneer, in all our poetic literature. Before him there was neither genuine blank verse nor a genuine tragedy in our language. After his arrival the way was prepared, the paths were made straight, for Shakespeare."[135]

BEN JONSON

Nicholas Rowe, the earliest Shakespearean biographer, claims it was the recommendation of William Shakespeare that gained Jonson's play *Every Man in His Humour* a performance in Shakespeare's company (the Lord Chamberlain's Men). In the cast of 1598, Shakespeare is listed first among the actors. Younger by eight years than Marlowe and Shakespeare, Jonson came to dominate the London theatre as both writer and theorist. He had strong ideas about how plays should be written: structurally they should follow a classical model and use characters made up of dominant personality traits or "humours."

133.   Riggs, 49. Interestingly, writing for a company of child actors never appealed to Shakespeare, though in addition to Marlowe, Ben Jonson wrote extensively for them.
134.   Ibid., 45.
135.   *Encyclopedia Britannica,* 11th ed. Vol 17.

Ben Jonson's theoretical bent would have served him well at a university. He was born in 1572 in Westminster, which was then a city separate from but adjacent to London. His petty school studies were at a small school at St. Martins-in-the-Field. As Kyd was lucky to go to Merchant Taylors' and study with Mulcaster, so Jonson had the good fortune to attend Westminster School where he studied with (and never forgot) the great William Camden.

Camden was an historian, writer, and antiquarian as well as teacher, who appreciated the astonishing outpouring of literature that marked his lifetime (1551-1623). In one of his histories (*Remaines of a Greater Worke concerning Britaine,* 1605), he wrote: "If I would come to [write about] our time, what a world could I present to you out of Sir Philip Sidney, Edmund Spenser, Samuel Daniel, Hugh Holland, Ben Johnson (sic), Thomas Campion, Michael Drayton, George Chapman, John Marston, William Shakespeare, and other most pregnant wits of these our times, whom succeeding ages may justly admire".[136]

Camden's pupil Jonson must have shown himself to be very bright, but though Jonson is reported to have been admitted to Saint John's College, Cambridge, it is thought he had to leave after only a few weeks for lack of funds. He left to help his stepfather who was working as a stonemason on some buildings at Lincoln's Inn. This was a great loss for Jonson. Instead of being a scholar at a distinguished university, he completed a seven-year apprenticeship to his bricklayer stepfather—a trade he hated so much he went off to war, after which he became a failed actor, and a most obstreperous Londoner: he was imprisoned for seditious

---

136.   Halliday, 81.

writing in a play called the *Isle of Dogs* and incarcerated again when he killed a fellow actor, Gabriel Spencer, in a duel. "O that Ben Jonson is a pestilent fellow" said one anonymous writer,[137] yet Jonson was a friend of William Shakespeare's, a successful playwright who enjoyed great aristocratic patronage, and one of the most formidable intellects of his day. Ironically, perhaps as a hedge against the vagaries of a literary profession, he was still paying his dues to the stonemasons' guild as late as 1611 when he was at the height of his success as a playwright.[138]

When analyzing the backgrounds of Elizabethan and Jacobean playwrights as summarized in F.E. Halliday's *A Shakespeare Companion,* we see that the most important Elizabethan/ Jacobean dramatists are almost equally divided between those with university educations and those with just a grammar school background.

University Graduates:

John Lyly*	c.1554-c.1606
Thomas Lodge*	c.1557-c.1625
George Peele*	c.1557-c.1596
Robert Greene*	1558- 1592
Barnabe Barnes	c.1559- 1609
George Chapman	c.1560- 1634

---

137. From *The Returne from Parnassus: or The Scourge of Simony* (1606). One of the three plays called The Parnassus Plays was presented at St. John's College, Cambridge University, 1601-02.

138. *Oxford Dictionary of National Biography,* "Jonson".

Samuel Daniel	c.1563- 1619
Christopher Marlowe*	1564- 1593
Thomas Nashe*	1567-c.1601
Thomas Middleton	c.1570- 1627
Thomas Heywood	1573- 1641
John Marston	c.1575- 1634
John Fletcher	1579- 1625
Philip Massinger	1583- 1640
Francis Beaumont	1584- 1616
John Ford	1586-c.1639

*The six known as the University Wits

Grammar School Background:

Robert Wilson	c.1550-c.1605
Thomas Kyd	1558- 1594
Henry Chettle	c.1560- 1607

Anthony Munday	c.1560- 1633
Michael Drayton	1563- 1631
William Shakespeare	1564- 1616
Richard Hathway	c.1570-c.1610
Samuel Rowley	c.1570-c.1630
Thomas Dekker	c.1572-c.1632
Benjamin Jonson	1572- 1637
John Day	c.1574-c.1640

(sent down from Cambridge before graduating)

William Haughton	c.1575- 1605
Cyril Tourneur	c.1575- 1626
Robert Daborne	1580- 1628
William Rowley	c.1580-c.1635
John Webster	c.1580-c.1630

Among the University Wits, Robert Greene bitterly disparaged his less educated colleagues, notably Shakespeare. But of the three most notable playwrights of the day (William Shakespeare, Christopher Marlowe, and Ben Jonson), two had only a grammar school education and all three came from working class backgrounds.

SELECTED BIBLIOGRAPHY

PRIMARY SOURCES

Ascham, Roger. *The Scholemaster, 1570*. Edited by R. J. Schoeck. Don Mills, Ont: Dent, 1966.

Aubrey, John. *Aubrey's Brief Lives.* Edited by Oliver Lawson Dick. Boston: David R. Godine, 1999.

Brinsley, John. *Ludus Literarius: or, The Grammar Schoole*. London: Printed for Thomas Man, 1612.

_____. *Pueriles Confabulatiunculae, 1617*. Menston, England: Scolar Press, 1971.

The Church of England. *The Book of Common Prayer, 1559; The Elizabethan Prayer Book*. Edited by John E. Booty. Charlottesville, VA: Published for the Folger Shakespeare Library by the University of Virginia Press, 2005.

Cicero, Marcus Tullius. *Ad Herennium:* http://penelope. uchicago. edu/Thayer/E/Roman/Texts/Rhetorica_ad_Herennium/1*.html

_____. *The Letters of Cicero*. Translated by Evelyn S. Shuckburgh. London: G. Bell and sons, 1899-1900. Ancient History Sourcebook: Cicero: Selected Letters. http://www. fordham.edu/halsall/ ancient/cicero-letters.asp

_____.*Topics.*http://www.classicpersuasion.org/pw/cicero/cicero-topics.htm

Clement, Francis. *The Petie Schole with an English Orthographie.* London: Thomas Vautrollier, 1587.

Coote, Edmund. *The English Schoolmaister, 1596*. London: A. Maxwell, 1670.

Cordier, Mathurin. *Corderii Colloquiorum centuria selecta, or, A select century of the Corderius' Colloquies; with an English translation, as literal as possible; designed for the use of beginners in the Latin tongue.* http://play.google.com/ books/reader?id=vvEpAAAAYAA J&printsec=frontcover&output=reader&hl=en&pg=GBS.PA16

Culman, Leonardum. *Sententiae Pueriles.* Translated by John Brinsley. London: H. Lownes for Thomas Man, 1612.

Henslowe's Diary, Walter W. Greg, ed. London: A. H. Bullen, 1904

Heywood, Thomas. *An Apology for Actors.* London: Nicholas Okes, 1612.

Hoole, Charles. *A New Discovery of the Old Art of Teaching Schoole.* 1636.

An Introduction of Algorisme, to learn to reckon with the Pen or With the Counters. Printed by John Awdeley. London: 1574.

Johnson, Ra. *The Scholars Guide from the Accidence to the University.* London: Tho. Pierrepont, 1665.

Lily, William. *A Short Introduction of Grammar Generallie to be Used.* London: Rebound by Robt. Lunow, 1557.

Mulcaster, Richard. *The First Part of the Elementerie which Entreateth Chefelie of the Right writing of our English tung.* London: Thomas Vautroullier, 1582.

_____. *Positions Concerning the Bringing Up of Children.* London: Thomas Vautroullier 1581.

Ovid. *Metamorphoses, The Arthur Golding Translation of 1567.* Philadelphia: Paul Dry Books, 2000.

Peacham, Henry. *The Compleat Gentleman* 1634. Oxford: Clarendon Press, 1906. http://openlibrary.org/books/ OL7050384M/ Compleat_gentleman_1634.

Plutarch. *The Lives of the Noble Grecians and Romans.* Translated out of Greek into French by James Amyot and out of French into English by Thomas North. Roland Baughman, ed. New York: The Heritage Press, 1941.

Recorde, Robert. *Arithmetick, or The Ground of Arts,* London: 1542, 1568. http://threesixty360.wordpress.com/tag/ robert-recorde.

_____. *The Whetstone of Witte.* London: 1557.

Sherry, Richard. *A Treatise of Schemes and Tropes.* London: John Day, 1550.

_____. *A Treatise of the Figures of Grammer and Rhetorike.* London: Totill, 1555.

Siliceus. *Arithmetica.* Paris: 1526.

Smith, John. *The Mysterie of Rhetorique Unveil'd.* London: E. Coptes for George Eversden, 1665.

Sternhold, Thomas, John Hopkins, and Others. *The Whole Book of Psalms Collected into English Metre,* 1549, 1562. Music for the Church of God, Copyright 2001. Page last modified on: 07/29/2004. http:// www.cgmusic.org/workshop/ oldver_frame.htm

Stockwood, John. A Plaine and Easie Laying open of the meaning and understanding of the Rules of Construction in the English Accidence. London: Frances Flower, 1590.

Suetonius. *The Lives of the Twelve Caesars.* http://penelope. uchicago. edu/Thayer/E/Roman/Texts/Suetonius/ 12Caesars/

Susenbrotus, Joannes. *Epigrammatum Libri II.* Nicol. Brillingerum, 1543.

_____. *Epitome troporum ac schematum et Grammaticorum & Rhetorume arte rhetorica libri tres* (Zurich, 1540).

Terence. *Flowers for Latin Speaking,* 1533. Compiled and translated by Nicholas Udall. Menston: The Scolar Press, 1972.

Webbe, Joseph. *Pueriles Confabulatiunculae,* 1627. Menston, England: The Scholar Press Limited, 1968.

Willis, R. *Mount Tabor. Or Private Exercises of a Penitent Sinner.* London: P. Stephens and C. Meredith for The Guilded Lion, 1639.

SECONDARY SOURCES

Abbott, Edwin A. *A Shakespearian Grammar: An Attempt to Illustrate Some of the Differences between Elizabethan and Modern English.* 3rd ed. London: Macmillan, 1870. Reprint, Mineola, N.Y.: Dover Publications, 2003.

Adams, Joseph Quincy. *A Life of William Shakespeare.* Boston: Houghton Mifflin Company, 1923.

Alexander, John R. "History of Accounting: Part 5 – Medieval Accounting." AccountancyStudents: The Online Accounting Community: Resources. http://www.accountancystudents. co.uk/resources/read/part_5_medieval_accounting/

Alexander, Jonathan J. G. *Medieval Illuminators and Their Methods of Work.* New Haven: Yale University Press, 1992.

Anders, H. R. D. *Shakespeare's Books: A Dissertation on Shakespeare's Reading and the Immediate Sources of His Works.* Berlin: Georg Reimer, 1904.

http://archive.org/stream/bookshakespeare00andeuoft#page/n3/ mode/2up

Arkins, Brian. "Heavy Seneca: his Influence on Shakespeare's Tragedies." *Classics Ireland* 2 (1995): 1-8. doi: 10.2307/ 25528274

Baldwin, Thomas W. *The Organization and Personnel of the Shakespearean Company.* Princeton: Princeton University Press, 1927.

_____. *Shakspere's Five-Act Structure.* Urbana: The University of Illinois Press, 1947.

_____. *William Shakspere's Petty School.* Urbana: The University of Illinois Press, 1943.

_____. *William Shakspere's Small Latine and Lesse Greeke.* Mansfield Centre, CT: Martino Publishing, 2005.

Bate, Jonathan. Soul of the Age: A Biography of the Mind of William Shakespeare. New York: Random House, 2009.

_____. "The Mirror of Life: How Shakespeare Conquered the World." *Harper's*, April 2007, 37-46.

Baynes, Thomas Spencer. "What Shakespeare Learnt at School." In *Shakespeare studies, and essay on English dictionaries.* London: Longmans, Green, and co., 1894. *Shakespeare Online.* http://www.shakespeare-online.com/ biography/whatdidshkread.html

Bearman, Robert, ed. *The History of an English Borough: Stratford Upon Avon.* Stroud, Gloucestershire: Sutton Pub., 1997.

Bennett, H. S. *English Books and Readers, 1558 to 1603: Being a Study in the History of the Book Trade in the Reign of Elizabeth I.* Cambridge: Cambridge University Press, 1989.

Bevington, David M. *Shakespeare and Biography.* Oxford: Oxford University Press, 2010.

Brown, John Howard. *Elizabethan Schooldays; An Account of the English Grammar Schools in the Second Half of the Sixteenth Century.* Oxford: B. Blackwell, 1933.

Chambers, E. K. *William Shakespeare: A Study of Facts and Problems.* Oxford: The Clarendon Press, 1930.

Chute, Marchette. *Shakespeare of London.* New York: E.P. Dutton, 1949.

Collins, Paul. *The Book of William: How Shakespeare's First Folio Conquered the World*. New York: Bloomsbury, 2009.

Connell, Charles. *They Gave Us Shakespeare: John Heminge & Henry Condell*. Boston: Oriel Press, 1982.

Cooper, Duff. *Sergeant Shakespeare*. New York: The Viking Press, 1950.

Cristensen, Ann C. *Absent Husbands: Separation Scenes in Early Modern English Domestic Drama*. Manuscript, 2011.

Crystal, David, and Ben Crystal. *Shakespeare's Words: A Glossary and Language Companion*. London: Penguin Books, 2002.

Duffin, Ross W. *Shakespeare's Songbook*. New York: W. W. Norton & Company, 2004.

Duncan-Jones, Katherine. *Ungentle Shakespeare*. London: Arden Shakespeare, 2001.

Durham, John W. "The Introduction of 'Arabic' Numerals in European Accounting." *The Accounting Historians Journal* 19 (December 1992): 25-55.

Dutton, Richard, ed *The Oxford Handbook of Early Modern Theatre*. Oxford: University Press, 2009.

Ebert, Emeline R. "A Few Observations on Robert Recorde and His 'Ground of Arts.'" *Mathematics Teacher* 30 (March 1937): 110-21.

Eccles, Mark. *Shakespeare in Warwickshire*. Madison: The University of Wisconsin Press, 1963.

Edwards, Anne-Marie. *Walking with William Shakespeare*. Madison, Wisconsin: Jones Books, 2005.

Elton, Charles Isaac. *William Shakespeare His Family and Friends*. Whitefish, Mt: Kessinger Publishing, 2003.

Enterline, Lynn. *Shakespeare's Schoolroom*. Philadelphia: University of Pennsylvania Press, 2012.

Fort, Alice B., and Herbert S. Kates. *Minute History of the Drama*. New York: Grosset & Dunlap, 1935.

Fripp, Edgar I. *Master Richard Quyny.*. London: Humphrey Milford, Oxford University Press, 1924.

_____. *Shakespeare's Stratford*. London: Oxford University Press, 1928.

Gale Encyclopedia of Biography, s.v."Robert Recorde" http:// www. answers.com/topic/robert-recorde

Gathorne-Hardy, Jonathan. *The Old School Tie*. New York: The Viking Press, 1977.

Gladwell, Malcolm. *Outliers*. New York: Little, Brown and Company, 2008.

Greenblatt, Stephen. *Will in the World: How Shakespeare Became Shakespeare*. New York, W.W. Norton, 2004.

Greer, Germaine. *Shakespeare's Wife*. New York: HarperCollins, 2007.

"The Guide to Life, the Universe and Everything *.s.v. "Robert Recorde–Mathematician."* http://H2g2.com/dna/h2g2/ A7269690

Gurr, Andrew. *The Shakespearean Stage, 1574-1642*. 4th ed. Cambridge: Cambridge University Press, 2008.

Hain, W. P. "Casting the Account." *Journal of Accounting Research* 5 (Autumn 1967): 154-63.

Halliday, F.E. *A Shakespeare Companion 1564-1964*. Baltimore: Penguin, 1964.

Harmon, William, and C. Hugh Holman. *A Handbook to Literature*. Upper Saddle River, N.J.: Prentice Hall, 2008.

Harrison, G.B. *Shakespeare's Fellows*. London: John Lane the Bodley Head LTD, 1923.

Hillar, Marian. Sebastian Castellio and the Struggle for Freedom of Conscience. In *Essays in the Philosophy of Humanism*, edited by D. R. Finch and M. Hillar. 10 (2002), 31-56. www.socinian.org/castellio.html

Honan, Park. *Shakespeare, A Life*. Oxford: Oxford University Press, 1998.

Jefferson, Lisa. *The Medieval Account Books of the Mercers of London*. Farnham, Surrey: Ashgate Pub., 2009.

Jones, Jeanne. *Family Life in Shakespeare's England Stratford-Upon-Avon 1570-1630*. Stroud, Gloucestershire: Sutton Pub.in association with the Shakespeare Birthplace Trust, 1996.

Joseph, Sister Miriam. C.S.C. *Shakespeare's Use of the Arts of Language*. Philadelphia: Paul Dry Books, 2005 (originally copyrighted 1947).

_____. *The Trivium*. Philadelphia: Paul Dry Books, 2002. (originally copyrighted 1937)

King Edward VI School, Stratford-Upon-Avon, Shakespeare's School. The Archive. King's Lynn, Norfolk: Bidles, Ltd. 2008.

Lanham, Richard A. *A Handlist of Rhetorical Terms*. Berkeley: University of California Press, 1968.

Lass, Abraham H, David Kiremidgian, and Ruth M. Goldstein. *The Wordsworth Dictionary of Classical and Literary Allusion*. Ware, Hertfordshire: Wordsworth Reference, 1994.

Long, Kenneth R. *The Music of the English Church*. London: Hodder & Stoughton, 1972.

Maguire, Laurie. *Where There's a Will There's a Way*. London: A Perigee Book, Penguin, 2006.

Marx, Steven. *Shakespeare and the Bible.* Oxford: Oxford University Press, 2000.

McDonald, Russ. *The Bedford Companion to Shakespeare.* Boston: Bedford Books, 1996.

Medieval Manuscript Manual. http://web.ceu.hu/medstud/ manual/ MMM/ink.html

Nickel, Joe. *Pen, Ink, and Evidence.* Lexington: The University Press of Kentucky, 1990.

Nicolson, Adam. God's Secretaries: The Making of the King James Bible. New York: Harper Perennial, 2004.

_____. "The Bible of King James." *National Geographic,* December 2011, pp. 36-51.

Noble, Richmond. *Shakespeare's Biblical Knowledge.* New York: Octagon Books, 1970.

Nuttall, A.D. *Shakespeare the Thinker.* New Haven: Yale University Press, 2007.

O'Dell, Leslie. *Shakespearean Language, A Guide for Actors and Students.* Westport, CT: Greenwood Press, 2002.

Olsen, Kirstin. *All Things Shakespeare, An Encyclopedia of Shakespeare's World.* Westport, CT: Greenwood Press, 2002.

Palfrey, Simon, and Tiffany Stern. *Shakespeare in Parts.* Oxford: Oxford University Press, 2008.

Palmer, Alan and Veronica. *Who's Who in Shakespeare's England.* New York: St. Martin's Press, 1981.

Parker, M. B. *Scribes, Scripts and Readers.* London: The Hambledon Press, 1991.

Partridge, Eric. *Shakespeare's Bawdy*. London: Routledge and Kegan, 1968.

Plimpton, George A. *The Education of Shakespeare*. Freeport, N.Y.: Books for Libraries Press, 1933.

Pogue, Kate Emery. *Shakespeare's Family*. Westport, Connecticut: Praeger, 2008.

_____. *Shakespeare's Figures of Speech*. New York: iUniverse, Inc. 2009.

_____. *Shakespeare's Friends*. Westport, Connecticut: Praeger, 2006.

Pohl, Frederick J. *Like to the Lark*. New York: Clarkson N. Potter, Inc., 1972.

Publications of the Dugdale Society, Volume III. Ed. By F. Wellstood. Stratford-Upon-Avon: Dugdale Society, 1921.

Riggs, David. *The World of Christopher Marlowe*. New York: Henry Holt and Company, 2004.

Rivington, Septimus. *The History of Tonbridge School*. London: Rivingtons, 1869.

Rolfe, William J. *Shakespeare the Boy*. Williamstown, Mass.: Corner House Publishers, 1982.

Rowse, A.L. *My View of Shakespeare*. London: Duckworth, 1996

_____. *Willliam Shakespeare, A Biography*. New York: Harper and Row, 1963.

Schoenbaum, Samuel. *William Shakespeare, a Compact Documentary Life*. New York: Oxford University Press, 1987.

Shakespeare, William. *Complete Works*. Edited by John Dover Wilson. Cambridge: Cambridge University Press, 1981.

Shapiro, James. *1599: A Year in the Life of William Shakespeare.* London: Faber and Faber, 2005.

_____. *Contested Will: Who Wrote Shakespeare?* New York: Simon and Schuster, 2010.

Stewart, Alan. *Shakespeare's Letters.* Oxford: Oxford University Press, 2008.

Stewart, Doug. *The Boy Who Would Be Shakespeare: A Tale of Forgery and Folly.* Philadelphia: Da Capo Press, 2010.

Stopes, Charlotte Carmichael. *Shakespeare's Warwickshire Contemporaries.* Stratford-Upon-Avon: Shakespeare Head Press, 1907.

Stowe, A. Monroe. *English Grammar Schools in the Reign of Queen Elizabeth.* New York: Teachers College, Columbia University, 1908.

Taplin, John. *Shakespeare's Country Families.* Warwick: Claridges of Warwick, 2011.

Vendler, Helen. *The Art of Shakespeare's Sonnets.* Cambridge: The Belknap Press of Harvard University Press, 1997.

Watson, Foster. *The Curriculum and Text-books of English Schools in the First Half of the Seventeenth Century.* London: Blades, East & Blades, 1903.

_____. *The English Grammar Schools to 1660: Their Curriculum and Practice.* Cambridge: University Press, 1908.

_____. *Tudor School Boy Life, the Dialogues of Juan Luis Vives.* London: J.M. Dent and Company, 1908.

_____. *Vives on Education,* Cambridge: University Press, 1913.

Wells, Stanley. *Shakespeare & Co.* New York: Pantheon Books, 2006.

Whitaker, Virgil K. *Shakespeare's Use of Learning.* San Marino, CA: The Huntington Library, 1953.

Wood, Clement E. *The Complete Rhyming Dictionary and Poet's Craft Book.* Garden City, NY: Doubleday and Company, 1936.

Wright, George T. *Shakespeare's Metrical Art.* Berkeley: University of California Press, 1988.

"Writing in Elizabethan Schools." Stratford Upon Avon: The Shakespeare Birthplace Trust, 2011.

INDEX